LIVING G[

DAILY
COOKBOOK

365 DAYS OF LIFE-CHANGING RECIPES

INSPIRED BY **DR. LIVINGOOD'S TEACHINGS** TO OVERCOME "SICK CARE" AND BUILD A HEALTHIER, LONGER LIFE NATURALLY

21-DAY MEAL PLAN INCLUDED

DEAN RICE

Catalog

Introduction

CHAPTER 1: Breakfasts

CHAPTER 2: Lunches

CHAPTER 3: Snacks

CHAPTER 4: Dinners

CHAPTER 5: Desserts

CHAPTER 6: Drinks

CHAPTER 7: The 21-Day Meal Plan

CHAPTER 8: Additional Resources

Introduction

🍇 HOW TO USE THIS COOKBOOK

Welcome to the **Living Good Daily Cookbook** - your new companion on the journey to a healthier lifestyle. This book is more than just a collection of recipes; it embodies a philosophy that food is not only fuel but also medicine that can enhance well-being and vitality. Crafted under the guidance of Dr. Livingood's teachings, it aims to shift your perspective on cooking and eating from routine to revolutionary.

This cookbook serves as a manual to navigate the world of healthy eating with ease. It introduces you to a way of cooking that intertwines nourishment with flavor, ensuring that every meal is a step toward optimal health. Whether you are just starting to cook or are experienced in the kitchen, the recipes here are designed to be accessible and adaptable, helping you to incorporate wholesome ingredients into your daily diet.

As you explore the pages, you will find that each recipe provides more than just instructions for preparing food. They are carefully formulated to highlight the health benefits of key ingredients, explaining how they contribute to your health. This approach is intended to deepen your understanding of nutrition, enabling you to make informed choices about what you eat.

The recipes are laid out with clarity and precision, making it easy to follow along and achieve consistent results. They include detailed descriptions of ingredients, step-by-step cooking methods, and suggestions for ingredient substitutions to accommodate dietary restrictions and preferences. This flexibility ensures that the recipes can be enjoyed by everyone, regardless of dietary needs.

In addition to the recipes, the cookbook features a comprehensive 21-Day Meal Plan. This plan is not just a list of meals but a curated guide that combines various recipes from the book into a structured eating plan. It helps you manage portions and nutritional intake, making it easier to maintain a balanced diet. Each week of the plan is designed to gradually introduce new recipes and ingredients, making the transition to healthier eating seamless and enjoyable.

Meal planning can often seem like a daunting task, but this book simplifies it. By following the 21-Day Meal Plan, you can take the guesswork out of what to prepare and ensure that you are getting a diverse range of nutrients. This plan also teaches meal prep techniques that save time, reduce waste, and keep your diet on track.

Cooking is as much about the process as it is about the outcome. This cookbook encourages you to embrace the art of cooking, to take pleasure in the tactile experience of handling ingredients, and to savor the aromas and tastes that fill your kitchen. It's about creating a ritual that celebrates food and its ability to heal and nourish both body and soul.

Lastly, make this cookbook your own. Write notes in the margins, experiment with flavors, and don't hesitate to tweak recipes to suit your taste. The **Living Good Daily Cookbook** is meant to be a dynamic tool that adapts to your lifestyle, helping you to forge a deeper connection with what you eat and how you live.

As you turn each page, let yourself be inspired by the possibility that lies in every recipe. Here's to cooking that's as good for the body as it is for the spirit - let's embark on this flavorful journey of transformation together.

THE PHILOSOPHY BEHIND "LIVING GOOD DAILY"

The Living Good Daily philosophy introduces a transformative approach to wellness that goes well beyond traditional dietary guidelines. It embraces a holistic lifestyle that enriches both mind and body and promotes an enriched relationship with food, urging us to see it as more than just sustenance. Rooted in Dr. Livingood's teachings, this approach advocates viewing food as a vital component of a comprehensive strategy for health and vitality.

Dr. Livingood's teachings emphasize the profound impact that our dietary choices have on our overall well-being. His approach blends ancient natural healing wisdom with modern scientific research, creating a balanced pathway that is accessible to everyone. It focuses on making informed choices that enhance health, improve mental clarity, and boost energy levels through the foods we consume daily.

At the heart of this philosophy is the concept of food as medicine. Dr. Livingood champions a diet rich in whole, unprocessed foods that nourish the body and help combat illness. This philosophy avoids restrictive diets and bland meals, instead celebrating the natural vibrancy and flavors of food that are nutritious and delicious. Foods in their most natural state fresh, vibrant, and brimming with life-giving nutrients are favored for both their health benefits and their taste.

Sustainability is a critical aspect of the Living Good Daily ethos. The philosophy underscores the idea that personal health is deeply interconnected with the health of our environment. It promotes sustainable eating practices such as local sourcing and seasonal eating, which support local economies and reduce our ecological footprints, ensuring that the foods we consume are beneficial for both us and the planet.

Holistic health is a cornerstone of Living Good Daily, viewing the body as an integrated system where physical, mental, and emotional health are interconnected. This approach goes beyond physical nourishment to include mental and spiritual well-being. It encourages practices that align our eating habits with our body's needs and promotes an overall balance that supports long-term health.

Education is pivotal in this philosophy. Living Good Daily is dedicated to demystifying the science behind healthy eating, making it accessible and understandable for everyone. By educating people on how different foods affect the body, the philosophy encourages a mindful approach to eating that focuses on the quality and origins of ingredients rather than just calorie counts.

Community involvement is also vital to the Living Good Daily philosophy. Sharing meals and knowledge about healthy practices helps strengthen community bonds and fosters a supportive environment for making healthier choices. This communal aspect enhances the journey toward health, making it a shared experience that extends beyond individual benefits.

The philosophy also embraces the emotional and psychological aspects of eating. Understanding that food can influence mood and mental states, Living Good Daily incorporates foods known for their mood-enhancing properties into the diet. This not only improves physical health but also contributes to emotional and mental well-being, creating a more balanced and joyful life.

Moreover, the philosophy recognizes the importance of adaptability and personalization in diet. Acknowledging that each person's body is unique, it allows for adjustments in dietary recommendations to suit individual health needs, preferences, and allergic sensitivities. This personalized approach ensures that everyone can benefit from the principles of Living Good Daily, regardless of their starting point.

Through the Living Good Daily philosophy, individuals are invited to transform their lives by adopting healthier habits that promote a vibrant and fulfilling existence. The philosophy aims not just to change how people eat but to reshape how they think about and engage with food. It encourages a proactive stance on health, fostering a lifestyle that is as enriching as it is healthful, with lasting impacts on personal health and the wider community.

NAVIGATING YOUR 21-DAY MEAL PLAN

Embarking on the 21-Day Meal Plan from the **Living Good Daily Cookbook** is more than just following a series of recipes; it's about embracing a journey toward transformative health and wellness. This plan is carefully designed not only to introduce you to a variety of nutritious foods but also to guide you through a meaningful change in how you approach eating and wellness.

The structure of the 21-Day Meal Plan is purposefully built to ease you into healthier eating habits. It starts with straightforward, nutritious meals that focus on basic, wholesome ingredients to help set a solid foundation without overwhelming you. As you progress through the days, the meals gradually become more varied and complex. This escalation introduces you to a broader spectrum of flavors and ingredients, each selected not only for their health benefits but also for their ability to bring joy and satisfaction to your dining table.

One of the core principles of this meal plan is its holistic approach to health. It goes beyond mere nutritional content to consider how food affects all aspects of your well-being, including mental clarity, emotional balance, and overall vitality. Each recipe is carefully chosen to contribute positively to your health, ensuring that every meal is an opportunity to enhance your life.

Flexibility is a cornerstone of the 21-Day Meal Plan. Recognizing that individual tastes and dietary requirements can vary widely, the plan is designed to be adaptable. You are encouraged to modify recipes according to your own needs and preferences, whether this means substituting ingredients, altering portion sizes, or adjusting cooking methods. This flexibility helps ensure that the meal plan can be comfortably integrated into any lifestyle, making it more likely that these new eating habits will stick long-term.

Educational insights accompany each recipe, offering detailed explanations about the nutritional benefits of the ingredients and the rationale behind each dish. This information aims to empower you with the knowledge to make informed dietary choices beyond the confines of the three-week plan. Understanding the 'why' behind your food can profoundly impact your relationship with eating, turning meal preparation and consumption into a thoughtful, intentional act.

The meal plan also encourages community interaction and support. Sharing your journey with others, whether through family meals, social media, or meal plan groups, can provide motivation and accountability. It reinforces that eating healthily is not just a personal goal but a communal experience that can foster deeper connections and shared learning.

Furthermore, the plan embraces the psychological aspects of eating by promoting mindful eating practices. This involves paying attention to how food looks, smells, and tastes, as well as recognizing your body's hunger and fullness signals. Mindful eating can transform your relationship with food from one of necessity to one of enjoyment and appreciation, making each meal a celebratory act of nourishing both body and soul.

Adaptability is another key feature of the meal plan. As you become more comfortable and confident with the initial recipes and principles, the plan encourages you to introduce new foods and experiment with different cooking techniques. This adaptability ensures that your diet remains dynamic and responsive to your evolving needs and preferences, which is essential for sustaining long-term health and wellness.

In essence, the 21-Day Meal Plan is not just a temporary diet but a gateway to lifelong healthy eating habits. It offers a comprehensive approach to improving your health, enhancing your culinary skills, and deepening your appreciation for the powerful role food plays in your life. By the end of the three weeks, you should feel empowered to continue making choices that support a vibrant, healthful lifestyle, equipped with the tools and knowledge to maintain this new path indefinitely. This plan is your stepping stone to a life where health, happiness, and delicious food go hand in hand.

Chapter 1
Breakfasts

 ## INTRODUCTION TO NUTRITIOUS MORNINGS

The start of each day offers a profound opportunity to influence our health and well-being positively. The "Nutritious Mornings" section of the **Living Good Daily Cookbook** focuses on elevating the first meal of the day, transforming it from a mundane task into a vital, nourishing ritual that sets the tone for the rest of the day. Recognizing breakfast as more than just a meal, this section is designed to energize, balance, and prepare you mentally and physically for your daily activities.

In today's hectic lifestyle, mornings are often rushed, leading many to skip breakfast or settle for quick, less nutritious options. Such choices can lead to a decline in mental sharpness, reduced energy levels, and a tendency to indulge in unhealthy snacks later in the day. The recipes in this cookbook challenge these habits by offering quick, easy-to-prepare dishes that do not compromise on nutritional value. They ensure that even the busiest individuals can have a wholesome, satisfying breakfast.

Each recipe meticulously combines proteins, fats, and carbohydrates to create well-rounded meals that sustain energy levels until the next meal. The selection of ingredients is intentional, focusing on whole foods that provide maximum nutritional benefits and flavors that delight the palate. The variety includes everything from savory egg dishes and refreshing smoothies to rich grain bowls and nourishing porridges, catering to diverse tastes and dietary preferences.

Moreover, this section encourages the inclusion of fruits and vegetables in your morning routine, extending breakfast's health benefits. These ingredients are rich in essential vitamins, minerals, and antioxidants, supporting overall health and preventing nutritional deficiencies. The inclusion of such diverse foods also ensures that breakfast never becomes monotonous but remains an enjoyable, creative part of your day.

The "Nutritious Mornings" recipes also emphasize the importance of understanding the source and quality of your food. By selecting ingredients that are organic and locally sourced when possible, you support sustainable agriculture and receive the benefits of fresher, more flavorful foods. This conscientious approach to selecting ingredients can deepen your connection to your food and its origins, enriching the overall eating experience.

Additionally, this cookbook section offers practical tips on meal preparation and planning. It provides strategies for making breakfast a feasible daily habit, such as preparing components of meals ahead of time or using leftovers creatively to save time and reduce waste. These tips make it easier to maintain a habit of a nutritious breakfast, even during the busiest mornings.

Ultimately, "Nutritious Mornings" is about more than just eating; it's about cultivating a morning ritual that enhances your health, enlivens your senses, and prepares you for the day ahead. By starting the day with a meal that is as nutritious as it is delicious, you set a positive pattern that can lead to improved health outcomes and a greater sense of daily satisfaction. This section invites you to rediscover the joy and importance of the morning meal, making it a cherished part of your routine that supports a vibrant, healthful life.

1. SUPERFOOD SMOOTHIE BOWL

Servings:
2

Prep Time:
10 minutes

Ingredients:

- 1 cup frozen mixed berries
- 1 frozen banana sliced
- 1/2 cup unsweetened Greek yogurt
- 1/2 cup spinach leaves
- 1 tablespoon chia seeds
- 1 tablespoon flaxseed meal
- 2 teaspoons honey (optional).

About the Dish

This superfood smoothie bowl is not just a breakfast but a burst of flavor and nutrition to kick-start your day. Packed with antioxidants from the mixed berries, it supports cellular health and reduces inflammation. Chia seeds and flaxseed meal provide fiber and omega-3 fatty acids to aid digestion and sustain energy levels. Spinach offers an incredible dose of vitamins and minerals, while Greek yogurt delivers protein for muscle repair and overall satiety. This vibrant, customizable dish is as refreshing as it is nourishing, ensuring your day begins on the healthiest note possible.

Step by Step Preparation

Begin by placing the frozen mixed berries, sliced frozen banana, Greek yogurt, and spinach leaves into a blender. Blend on high until the mixture is smooth and creamy, pausing occasionally to scrape down the sides for even blending. Adjust the thickness by adding a splash of water or milk if needed. Once blended, pour the smoothie mixture into serving bowls and spread it evenly using the back of a spoon. Add your favorite toppings, such as sliced fresh fruit, granola, or additional chia seeds, to enhance flavor and texture. Serve immediately and enjoy the wholesome goodness.

2. OVERNIGHT CHIA & OATS PARFAIT

Servings:
2

Prep Time:
5 minutes (plus overnight chilling)

Ingredients:

- 1/2 cup rolled oats
- 1/4 cup chia seeds
- 2 cups almond milk
- 1 teaspoon vanilla extract
- 2 teaspoons maple syrup
- 1/2 cup fresh fruit for topping
- 1/4 cup granola for garnish.

About the Dish

This overnight chia and oats parfait is a testament to the power of preparation. Combining the creaminess of soaked oats with the nutritional density of chia seeds, this breakfast fuels your day with fiber, protein, and omega-3 fatty acids. Almond milk adds a nutty richness, while the fresh fruit and granola provide natural sweetness and crunch. This dish isn't just practical for busy mornings; it's also a delightful way to enjoy layers of flavors and textures while nourishing your body.

Step by Step Preparation

In a large mixing bowl, combine the rolled oats, chia seeds, almond milk, vanilla extract, and maple syrup. Stir thoroughly to ensure the chia seeds are evenly distributed and begin absorbing the liquid. Cover the bowl and refrigerate overnight. In the morning, give the mixture a good stir to loosen it up. Divide the oat and chia mixture into serving glasses or bowls, layering with fresh fruit for bursts of color and flavor. Top each parfait with granola for an added crunch, and serve immediately.

3. QUINOA & BERRY BREAKFAST BOWL

Servings:
2

Prep Time:
15 minutes

Ingredients:

- 1 cup cooked quinoa
- 1/2 cup mixed berries
- 1/4 cup unsweetened coconut milk
- 1 tablespoon honey
- 1 tablespoon sliced almonds
- 1 tablespoon shredded coconut.

About the Dish

The quinoa and berry breakfast bowl redefines breakfast by incorporating this nutrient-rich grain. Quinoa is a complete protein, making it a perfect choice for sustained energy throughout the morning. Mixed berries deliver antioxidants and vibrant flavor, while the coconut milk provides creaminess without adding excess calories. Almonds and shredded coconut contribute texture and healthy

fats, creating a breakfast that is as wholesome as it is satisfying.

Step by Step Preparation

Start by reheating the cooked quinoa if it's not freshly prepared. In a small saucepan, warm the coconut milk and stir in the honey until fully dissolved. Mix the warm quinoa with the sweetened coconut milk in a serving bowl. Top with mixed berries, sliced almonds, and shredded coconut, creating a visually appealing and flavorful meal. Drizzle with additional honey if desired, and serve immediately for a warm, energizing breakfast.

4. AVOCADO TOAST WITH POACHED EGGS

Servings:
2

Prep Time:
15 minutes

Ingredients:

- 4 slices whole-grain bread
- 2 ripe avocados mashed
- 4 eggs
- 1 tablespoon white vinegar
- salt and pepper to taste
- red chili flakes or everything bagel seasoning for garnish.

About the Dish

Avocado toast with poached eggs is a perfect combination of simplicity and nutrition. Avocados provide heart-healthy monounsaturated fats and an array of vitamins, while poached eggs contribute high-quality protein for sustained energy. Whole-grain bread adds fiber, making this a well-balanced, satisfying breakfast. The seasoning adds a burst of flavor, ensuring every bite is as delightful as it is nourishing.

Step by Step Preparation

Toast the slices of whole-grain bread to your preferred level of crispiness. Meanwhile, bring a pot of water to a gentle simmer and add the white vinegar. Crack each egg into a small bowl and carefully slide it into the simmering water. Cook for three to four minutes until the whites are set and the yolks remain runny. Spread the mashed avocado evenly across the toasted bread slices and season lightly with salt and pepper. Top each piece with a poached egg, then sprinkle with chili flakes or everything bagel seasoning. Serve immediately for a wholesome and flavorful start to your day.

5. SWEET POTATO AND GREENS HASH

Servings:
2

Prep Time:
20 minutes

Ingredients:

- 1 medium sweet potato diced
- 1 cup kale chopped
- 1/2 red onion diced
- 1 clove garlic minced
- 2 eggs, 2 tablespoons olive oil
- salt and pepper to taste.

About the Dish

Sweet potato and greens hash is a warm, hearty breakfast packed with flavor and nutrients. Sweet potatoes provide complex carbohydrates for last-ing energy and a natural sweetness that balances perfectly with the earthy kale. Red onion and garlic infuse the dish with aromatic depth, while eggs complete the meal with high-quality protein. This dish is as satisfying as it is wholesome, making it an ideal start to any day.

Step by Step Preparation

Heat olive oil in a large skillet over medium heat. Add the diced sweet potatoes and cook for 8 to 10 minutes, stirring occasionally, until tender and slightly crisped. Stir in the diced red onion and minced garlic, cooking for another 3 minutes until fragrant. Add the chopped kale to the skillet, cooking just until wilted. Push the hash to one side of the skillet and crack the eggs into the empty space. Cover the skillet and cook for 3 to 4 minutes, or until the egg whites are set but the yolks are still runny. Season with salt and pepper to taste and serve hot.

6. ALMOND BUTTER PANCAKES

Servings:
2

Prep Time:
15 minutes

Ingredients:

- 1 cup almond flour
- 2 eggs
- 1/4 cup almond butter
- 1/4 cup almond milk
- 1 teaspoon vanilla extract
- 1 teaspoon baking powder
- 1 tablespoon maple syrup
- coconut oil for cooking.

About the Dish

Almond butter pancakes are a delicious and nutritious gluten-free twist on a breakfast favorite. Made with almond flour and almond butter, these pancakes are rich in protein and healthy fats that keep you full and satisfied. The natural sweetness of maple syrup and the creamy texture of almond milk elevate the flavor, making these pancakes an indulgent yet guilt-free treat for any morning.

Step by Step Preparation

In a mixing bowl, whisk together the almond flour, baking powder, eggs, almond butter, almond milk, vanilla extract, and maple syrup until smooth. Heat a skillet over medium heat and add a small amount of coconut oil. Pour the batter onto the skillet in small circles and cook for 2 to 3 minutes until bubbles form on the surface. Flip the pancakes and cook for another 2 minutes until golden brown. Serve warm with additional almond butter, maple syrup, or your favorite toppings.

7. GREEN DETOX SMOOTHIE

Servings:
2

Prep Time:
5 minutes

Ingredients:

- 1 cup spinach
- 1/2 cucumber chopped
- 1 green apple cored and sliced
- 1/2 avocado
- 1 tablespoon lemon juice
- 1 cup coconut water.

About the Dish

The green detox smoothie is a light yet powerful way to start your day. Spinach and cucumber provide hydration and essential vitamins, while avocado adds creaminess and heart-healthy fats. The green apple contributes a refreshing sweetness, and the coconut water replenishes electrolytes for optimal hydration. This smoothie is perfect for anyone seeking a nutritious, energizing, and refreshing start to the morning.

Step by Step Preparation

Add the spinach, chopped cucumber, green apple slices, avocado, lemon juice, and coconut water to a blender. Blend on high until smooth and creamy, adjusting the consistency with more coconut water if necessary. Pour the smoothie into glasses and serve immediately for a revitalizing start to your day.

8. ENERGIZING NUT AND SEED GRANOLA

Servings:
8

Prep Time:
15 minutes (plus 20 minutes baking)

Ingredients:

- 2 cups rolled oats
- 1/2 cup chopped almonds
- 1/2 cup sunflower seeds
- 1/4 cup chia seeds
- 1/4 cup flaxseed meal
- 1/3 cup honey
- 1/4 cup coconut oil melted
- 1 teaspoon cinnamon
- 1/2 cup dried cranberries.

About the Dish

This energizing nut and seed granola is the ultimate breakfast or snack for those looking for a nutrient-dense start to their day. Packed with heart-healthy fats, protein, and fiber, it keeps you full and energized for hours. The combination of oats, nuts, and seeds delivers a satisfying crunch, while the touch of honey and dried cranberries adds natural sweetness. Whether enjoyed with milk, yogurt, or on its own, this granola is a versatile and healthful option.

Step by Step Preparation

Begin by preheating your oven to 325°F and lining a large baking sheet with parchment paper. In a large mixing bowl, combine the rolled oats, chopped almonds, sunflower seeds, chia seeds, flaxseed meal, and cinnamon. In a separate bowl, whisk together the melted coconut oil and honey until fully combined. Pour the wet mixture over the dry ingredients and stir thoroughly to ensure everything is evenly coated. Spread the mixture in a single layer on the prepared baking sheet. Place the tray in the oven and bake for 20 minutes, stirring halfway through to ensure even browning. Remove from the oven when golden and fragrant. Allow the granola to cool completely on the tray before stirring in the dried cranberries. Transfer to an airtight container for storage and enjoy with your favorite yogurt or milk.

9. SAVORY SPINACH AND FETA MUFFINS

Servings:
12 muffins

Prep Time:
15 minutes (plus 25 minutes baking)

Ingredients:

- 2 cups whole wheat flour
- 1 teaspoon baking powder
- 1/2 teaspoon baking soda
- 3 eggs
- 1/2 cup olive oil
- 1/2 cup plain Greek yogurt
- 1 cup spinach chopped
- 1/2 cup feta cheese crumbled
- salt and pepper to taste.

About the Dish

These savory spinach and feta muffins are a delicious and convenient option for busy mornings. Packed with the goodness of spinach and the tangy flavor of feta, they offer a satisfying balance of nutrients and flavor. The whole wheat flour adds fiber, while the Greek yogurt keeps the muffins moist and fluffy. Perfect for breakfast on the go or as a light snack, these muffins are a wholesome addition to your morning routine.

Step by Step Preparation

Preheat your oven to 350°F and prepare a muffin tin by lining it with paper liners or lightly greasing it with oil. In a large bowl, combine the whole wheat flour, baking powder, and baking soda, mixing well to evenly distribute the leavening agents. In a separate bowl, whisk the eggs until frothy, then stir in the olive oil and Greek yogurt until smooth. Gradually incorporate the wet ingredients into the dry mixture, stirring until just combined. Be careful not to overmix, as this can make the muffins dense. Gently fold in the chopped spinach and crumbled feta cheese, seasoning with salt and pepper to taste. Divide the batter evenly among the muffin cups, filling each about two-thirds full. Bake in the preheated oven for 20 to 25 minutes, or until a toothpick inserted into the center of a muffin comes out clean. Allow the muffins to cool in the tin for 5 minutes before transferring them to a wire rack to cool completely. Serve warm or store in an airtight container for up to three days.

10. TOFU SCRAMBLE WITH TURMERIC

Servings:
2

Prep Time:
15 minutes

Ingredients:

- 1 block firm tofu crumbled
- 1 tablespoon olive oil
- 1/2 teaspoon turmeric
- 1/4 teaspoon paprika
- 1/2 teaspoon garlic powder
- 1/2 cup diced bell peppers
- 1/2 cup spinach chopped
- salt and pepper to taste.

About the Dish

This tofu scramble with turmeric is a plant-based alternative to scrambled eggs that is just as satisfying and packed with flavor. Tofu provides a great source of plant-based protein, while turmeric adds a vibrant yellow hue and powerful anti-inflammatory properties. The addition of bell peppers and spinach ensures you get a dose of essential vitamins and minerals in every bite. This dish is light yet hearty, making it a perfect breakfast or brunch option.

Step by Step Preparation

Start by preparing the tofu by draining it and crumbling it into small pieces with your hands or a fork. Heat a skillet over medium heat and add the olive oil. Once the oil is hot, add the diced bell peppers and cook for about 3 minutes until they soften. Add the crumbled tofu to the skillet and sprinkle with turmeric, paprika, and garlic powder. Stir well to coat the tofu evenly with the spices. Cook for 5 minutes, stirring occasionally, to allow the flavors to meld and the tofu to heat through. Add the chopped spinach and cook for another 2 minutes, just until the spinach wilts. Season with salt and pepper to taste, then transfer to serving plates. Pair the scramble with whole-grain toast or avocado slices for a balanced, protein-packed breakfast.

Chapter 2
Lunches

 INTRODUCTION TO MIDDAY MEALS

Lunch is far more than just a break in the day. It is an essential opportunity to nourish your body and restore your energy, setting the tone for how you will feel and perform in the hours ahead. The "Midday Meals" section of the Living Good Daily Cookbook is thoughtfully curated to transform this often-overlooked meal into a cornerstone of health and vitality. These recipes aim to bridge the gap between convenience and nourishment, offering meals that are easy to prepare, satisfying, and full of flavor.

In today's fast-paced world, lunch is often reduced to a moment of compromise. Many people resort to processed convenience foods, quick takeout, or skip lunch entirely, thinking it saves time. However, these choices often lead to fatigue, irritability, and cravings for unhealthy snacks later in the day. The recipes in this section are designed to change that narrative entirely. They provide meals that nourish your body with proteins, healthy fats, and complex carbohydrates, ensuring you feel full and energized without the heavy feeling or sugar crash that comes from less balanced meals.

One of the guiding principles of the Living Good Daily Cookbook is to make healthy eating both approachable and sustainable. The "Midday Meals" section embodies this philosophy by offering a variety of recipes that fit seamlessly into busy lifestyles. Whether you work from home, commute to an office, or juggle family responsibilities, this section provides options that are quick to assemble, easy to store, and perfect for meal prepping. The goal is to simplify lunch without sacrificing nutrition or taste, showing that healthy meals are achievable no matter how hectic your schedule may be.

This section also celebrates variety and creativity. Lunch should never feel repetitive or uninspiring, and these recipes introduce diverse flavors, textures, and cuisines. From crisp, refreshing salads with vibrant dressings to hearty grain bowls filled with colorful ingredients, the "Midday Meals" section inspires you to think beyond ordinary sandwiches. If you are craving something warm and comforting, you will find recipes for soups and stews that are both simple to prepare and deeply satisfying.

Each recipe is designed to deliver a balanced combination of nutrients. Proteins like lean meats, legumes, and plant-based alternatives are paired with fiber-rich vegetables and whole grains to keep your energy steady throughout the day. Healthy fats from avocados, nuts, and seeds are thoughtfully incorporated to promote brain health and keep you feeling full longer. Every ingredient is carefully chosen to provide maximum nutritional benefit while enhancing the overall flavor of the dish.

Practicality is another key focus of this section. Many of the recipes are ideal for meal prepping, making it easy to have healthy options ready to go throughout the week. Preparing components like roasted vegetables, cooked grains, or homemade dressings in advance simplifies the process of putting together a wholesome lunch, even on the busiest days. These recipes empower you to plan ahead, eliminating the guesswork and temptation of less nutritious options during your workday.

Lunch is not just about feeding your body; it is also about resetting and recharging your mind. The Living Good Daily philosophy encourages mindfulness and enjoyment during your lunch break. Taking the time to prepare and savor a wholesome meal allows you to step away from the stress of the day and focus on self-care. When you approach lunch with intention, it becomes more than a routine. It becomes an opportunity to nourish yourself in every sense of the word, promoting both physical health and emotional well-being.

The recipes in this section also prioritize adaptability. Everyone has unique tastes and dietary needs, so the dishes can be customized to suit your preferences. Whether you prefer plant-based options, need gluten-free alternatives, or want to incorporate more vegetables into your meals, the recipes are flexible enough to accommodate. This ensures that the "Midday Meals" section is inclusive and enjoyable for everyone.

Lunch is also a time for connection, whether it is with coworkers, family, or friends. Sharing a thoughtfully prepared meal can foster moments of togetherness and strengthen relationships. The recipes in this section are easy to scale, making them ideal for group settings or family meals. By preparing and enjoying lunch together, you not only nourish your bodies but also create shared experiences that build bonds and memories.

The "Midday Meals" section of the Living Good Daily Cookbook is an invitation to rethink lunch entirely. It challenges the notion that lunch is a quick or forgettable meal, instead presenting it as a daily opportunity to care for yourself, explore new flavors, and embrace mindfulness. By prioritizing high-quality ingredients and simple preparation techniques, these recipes help you create lunches that are satisfying, nourishing, and deeply enjoyable.

When you transform your lunch routine into something deliberate and fulfilling, you take a meaningful step toward living well every day. Each recipe in this section is a reminder that healthy eating does not have to be complicated. It can be vibrant, exciting, and deeply rewarding. As you explore these midday inspirations, you will discover how nourishing your body at lunch can elevate your entire day, helping you live with greater energy, focus, and joy.

11. KALE CAESAR SALAD WITH CHICKPEA CROUTONS

Servings:
2

Prep Time:
20 minutes

Ingredients:

- 4 cups chopped kale
- 1/2 cup grated Parmesan cheese
- 1 cup canned chickpeas drained and rinsed
- 2 tablespoons olive oil
- 1 teaspoon garlic powder
- salt and pepper to taste
- Caesar dressing to taste.

About the Dish

This Kale Caesar Salad reimagines the classic Caesar with a nutritious twist. Kale, rich in vitamins K, A, and C, replaces traditional romaine for an antioxidant boost. The chickpea croutons add a delightful crunch and a punch of protein, making this salad not just a side dish but a fulfilling meal. The creamy Caesar dressing ties all the flavors together, while Parmesan adds a savory note that perfectly complements the earthy kale.

Step by Step Preparation

Begin by preheating your oven to 375°F for the chickpea croutons. Toss the drained chickpeas with olive oil, garlic powder, salt, and pepper. Spread them on a baking sheet and bake for about 15-20 minutes, or until crispy. Meanwhile, wash and thoroughly dry the kale, then chop it into bite-sized pieces. Place the kale in a large mixing bowl, add the Caesar dressing, and massage gently to soft-

en the leaves. Once the chickpeas are crispy and golden, let them cool slightly before adding them to the salad. Toss the kale with grated Parmesan cheese and top with the warm chickpea croutons. Serve immediately for the best texture and flavor.

12. QUINOA TABBOULEH WITH FRESH HERBS

Servings:
4

Prep Time:
15 minutes

Ingredients:

- 2 cups cooked quinoa
- 1 cup chopped fresh parsley
- 1/2 cup chopped fresh mint
- 1/4 cup finely chopped red onion
- 1 cup diced tomatoes
- 1/4 cup lemon juice
- 1/4 cup olive oil
- salt and pepper to taste.

About the Dish

Quinoa Tabbouleh with Fresh Herbs is a fresh and light salad that's perfect for any season. This dish blends fluffy quinoa with vibrant fresh herbs like parsley and mint, which not only add flavor but also a range of health benefits. The red onion and tomatoes provide crunch and sweetness, while a simple dressing of lemon juice and olive oil dresses the salad without overpowering the delicate flavors.

Step by Step Preparation

Start by cooking the quinoa according to package instructions and allow it to cool. In a large bowl, combine the cooled quinoa with chopped parsley, mint, red onion, and diced tomatoes. In a small bowl, whisk together the lemon juice, olive oil, salt, and pepper to create a light dressing. Pour the dressing over the quinoa mixture and toss to combine thoroughly. Adjust seasoning to taste. Refrigerate the tabbouleh for at least an hour before serving to allow the flavors to meld. Serve chilled or at room temperature.

13. SWEET CORN AND AVOCADO SALAD

Servings:
4

Prep Time:
10 minutes

Ingredients:

- 3 cups cooked sweet corn kernels
- 2 ripe avocados diced
- 1/2 red bell pepper diced
- 1/4 cup finely chopped red onion
- 2 tablespoons chopped cilantro
- juice of 1 lime
- 2 tablespoons olive oil
- salt and pepper to taste.

About the Dish

Sweet Corn and Avocado Salad is a vibrant and refreshing dish that pairs the natural sweetness of corn with the creamy texture of avocado. The addition of red bell pepper and red onion adds a crisp texture and a pop of color, while cilantro and lime juice bring a zesty freshness that makes this salad a perfect side dish or a light standalone meal.

Step by Step Preparation

In a large bowl, combine the cooked sweet corn kernels, diced avocados, diced red bell pepper, and chopped red onion. Add the chopped cilantro for an aromatic lift. In a small bowl, whisk together lime juice, olive oil, salt, and pepper to create a dressing. Drizzle the dressing over the salad ingredients and gently toss to coat everything evenly. Be careful to mix gently to keep the avocado pieces intact. Adjust the seasoning as needed, and serve immediately to enjoy the freshness of the ingredients.

14. MEDITERRANEAN VEGGIE WRAP

Servings:
4

Prep Time:
20 minutes

Ingredients:

- 4 whole wheat wraps
- 1 cup hummus
- 1 cucumber sliced
- 1 tomato sliced
- 1/4 cup sliced red onions
- 1/2 cup sliced bell peppers
- 1 cup spinach leaves
- 1/4 cup feta cheese crumbled
- 1/4 cup olives sliced
- salt and pepper to taste.

About the Dish

The Mediterranean Veggie Wrap is a hearty, flavorful meal that packs a variety of textures and tastes into every bite. The base of hummus provides a creamy texture and protein, while the assortment of vegetables ensures a crunch in every bite. Feta cheese adds a tangy sharpness, and olives bring a briny depth that ties all the flavors together beautifully.

Step by Step Preparation

Lay out the whole wheat wraps on a clean surface. Spread a generous layer of hummus over each wrap, leaving a small border around the edges. Layer the cucumber, tomato, red onions, bell peppers, and spinach leaves on top of the hummus. Sprinkle crumbled feta cheese and sliced olives over the vegetables. Season with salt and pepper to taste. Carefully roll each wrap tightly to enclose the fillings, then slice in half diagonally. Serve immediately or wrap tightly in foil to take on the go.

15. SPICY LENTIL AND SWEET POTATO SOUP

Servings:
4

Prep Time:
30 minutes

Ingredients:

- 1 tablespoon olive oil
- 1 large sweet potato peeled and diced
- 1 cup red lentils rinsed
- 1 onion chopped
- 2 cloves garlic minced
- 4 cups vegetable broth
- 1 teaspoon ground cumin
- 1/2 teaspoon chili powder
- salt and pepper to taste
- 1/4 cup chopped fresh cilantro for garnish.

About the Dish

Spicy Lentil and Sweet Potato Soup is a comforting and filling dish that combines the sweetness of sweet potatoes with the heartiness of lentils. Infused with spices like cumin and chili powder, this soup offers warmth and depth of flavor. It's an ideal meal for colder days or whenever you need a nutritious boost.

Step by Step Preparation

Heat olive oil in a large pot over medium heat. Add the chopped onion and minced garlic, sautéing until the onion becomes translucent. Add the diced sweet potato and rinsed red lentils to the pot, stirring to combine. Pour in the vegetable broth and bring the mixture to a boil. Reduce the heat and let simmer for about 20 minutes, or until the lentils and sweet potatoes are tender. Add the ground cumin and chili powder, and season with salt and pepper. Use an immersion blender to partially blend the soup if a thicker consistency is desired, or leave it chunky for texture. Serve hot, garnished with chopped cilantro.

16. BROCCOLI AND ALMOND SOUP

Servings:
4

Prep Time:
25 minutes

Ingredients:

- 2 tablespoons olive oil
- 1 onion chopped
- 2 cloves garlic minced
- 4 cups broccoli florets

- 1/4 cup ground almonds
- 4 cups vegetable broth
- salt and pepper to taste
- almond slivers for garnish.

About the Dish

Broccoli and Almond Soup is a creamy, comforting blend that marries the earthy flavor of fresh broccoli with the rich, nutty undertones of almonds. This soup is an excellent source of vitamins and fiber, providing a healthy boost to your day. The ground almonds not only contribute a creamy texture without dairy but also add valuable protein and heart-healthy fats, making this dish wonderfully nourishing. It's perfect for those seeking a light yet satisfying meal, with the subtle flavors perfectly balanced to delight the palate.

Step by Step Preparation

Start by heating the olive oil in a large pot over medium heat. Add the chopped onion and minced garlic, sautéing until the onion becomes translucent and fragrant. Introduce the broccoli florets to the pot, stirring frequently, until they begin to soften and turn a vibrant green, about 5 minutes. Stir in the ground almonds, mixing well to combine with the broccoli. Pour in the vegetable broth, and season with salt and pepper to taste. Bring the soup to a boil, then reduce the heat and let it simmer for about 15-20 minutes, or until the broccoli is completely tender. Use an immersion blender to puree the soup directly in the pot until smooth. If the soup is too thick, adjust the consistency with a bit more broth or water until you reach your desired thickness. Serve the soup hot, garnished with a sprinkle of almond slivers for added texture and a touch of elegance.

17. GRILLED CHICKEN AND HUMMUS FLATBREAD

Servings:
4

Prep Time:
30 minutes

Ingredients:

- 4 flatbreads
- 2 chicken breasts grilled and sliced
- 1 cup hummus
- 1 cucumber sliced
- 1 tomato sliced
- 1 red onion thinly sliced
- 1/4 cup feta cheese crumbled
- 2 tablespoons olive oil
- salt and pepper to taste.

About the Dish

Grilled Chicken and Hummus Flatbread is a delightful fusion of Mediterranean flavors, featuring juicy grilled chicken, creamy hummus, and fresh, crisp vegetables all atop a soft flatbread. This dish is an excellent blend of protein, fiber, and healthy fats, providing a balanced and satisfying meal. The hummus adds a smooth texture and garlicky punch, which complements the smoky chicken perfectly, while the fresh vegetables provide crunch and freshness, and the feta adds a tangy sharpness that ties all the flavors together.

Step by Step Preparation

Begin by preheating your grill or grill pan over medium heat. Brush the chicken breasts with olive oil and season with salt and pepper to taste. Grill the chicken for about 5-7 minutes on each side or until they have nice grill marks and the internal temperature reaches 165°F. Let the chicken rest for a few minutes before slicing it thinly. To assemble the flatbreads, spread a generous layer of hummus over each flatbread. Arrange the sliced chicken evenly across the hummus. Top with cucumber slices, tomato slices, and red onion. Sprinkle crumbled feta cheese over the top and drizzle with a little olive oil. Finally, season with a bit more salt and pepper. Serve immediately, or if preferred, briefly grill the assembled flatbreads for 1-2 minutes on each side to warm through.

18. SUSHI BOWL WITH BROWN RICE

Servings:
4

Prep Time:
30 minutes

Ingredients:

- 2 cups cooked brown rice
- 1 cup diced cucumber
- 1 cup shredded carrots
- 1 avocado sliced
- 8 ounces cooked shrimp or smoked salmon
- 1/2 cup sliced green onions
- 1/4 cup soy sauce
- 1 tablespoon sesame oil
- 1 teaspoon wasabi paste
- 1 tablespoon pickled ginger
- sesame seeds for garnish.

About the Dish

The Sushi Bowl with Brown Rice brings all the beloved flavors of sushi into an easy-to-make, deconstructed bowl. Using hearty brown rice as the base, this dish not only provides a good source of fiber but also offers a chewy texture that complements the fresh, crisp vegetables and the rich, savory seafood. The combination of creamy avocado, crunchy cucumber, and carrots with either tender shrimp or smoky salmon makes for a satisfying meal that's as nutritious as it is delicious. Drizzled with a simple dressing of soy sauce and sesame oil and topped with wasabi and pickled ginger, each bite offers a burst of authentic sushi flavor.

Step by Step Preparation

Begin by evenly distributing the cooked brown rice into four bowls. Arrange the diced cucumber, shredded carrots, and slices of avocado neatly over the rice. Add the cooked shrimp or smoked salmon to each bowl. Sprinkle sliced green onions across the top for a sharp, fresh flavor contrast. In a small bowl, mix together the soy sauce, sesame oil, and wasabi paste until well combined. Drizzle this dressing over each bowl, ensuring each ingredient gets a touch of flavor. Garnish with pickled ginger and a sprinkle of sesame seeds for an extra pop of texture and flavor. Serve immediately, allowing everyone to mix their bowl to their liking, combining all the vibrant ingredients for a truly satisfying meal.

19. COLD NOODLE SALAD WITH PEANUT SAUCE

Servings:
4

Prep Time:
20 minutes

Ingredients:

- 8 ounces soba noodles
- 1 red bell pepper thinly sliced

- 1 cucumber julienned
- 1 carrot julienned
- 1/4 cup chopped cilantro
- 1/4 cup crushed peanuts
- **for the sauce:** 1/3 cup peanut butter
- 2 tablespoons soy sauce
- 1 tablespoon lime juice
- 1 tablespoon honey
- 1 clove garlic minced
- 1 teaspoon grated ginger
- water as needed to thin the sauce.

About the Dish

Cold Noodle Salad with Peanut Sauce is a vibrant, flavor-packed dish that's perfect for warm weather meals or any time you crave something light yet fulfilling. The noodles are dressed in a creamy, spicy peanut sauce that coats each strand with a rich, savory flavor. Crisp vegetables like red bell pepper, cucumber, and carrot provide a crunchy texture and lots of nutrients, while cilantro adds a fresh, herby brightness. Topped with crushed peanuts, this dish is a delightful blend of textures and flavors that's both refreshing and satisfying.

Step by Step Preparation

Cook the soba noodles according to package instructions, then rinse under cold water and drain thoroughly. In a large mixing bowl, combine the chilled noodles with thinly sliced red bell pepper, julienned cucumber, and carrot. Toss these ingredients to mix. In a separate small bowl, whisk together the peanut butter, soy sauce, lime juice, honey, minced garlic, and grated ginger. Add water a tablespoon at a time until the sauce reaches a pourable consistency. Pour the peanut sauce over the noodle mixture and toss to coat everything evenly. Garnish the salad with chopped cilantro and crushed peanuts for an extra layer of flavor

and crunch. Serve the salad chilled, ideally letting it sit for a few minutes before serving to allow the flavors to meld together.

20. ROASTED VEGGIE AND QUINOA SALAD

Servings:	Prep Time:
4	45 minutes

Ingredients:

- 1 cup quinoa
- 2 cups vegetable broth
- 1 zucchini chopped
- 1 red bell pepper chopped
- 1 yellow bell pepper chopped
- 1/2 red onion chopped
- 2 tablespoons olive oil
- salt and pepper to taste
- 1/4 cup feta cheese crumbled
- 1/4 cup balsamic vinaigrette.

About the Dish

Roasted Veggie and Quinoa Salad is a hearty, colorful dish packed with nutrients and flavors. The quinoa serves as a high-protein base, while a medley of roasted vegetables adds depth and richness with their caramelized edges and tender textures. The addition of feta cheese provides a creamy, tangy counterpoint to the earthy flavors of the vegetables, and a drizzle of balsamic vinaigrette brings a bright, tangy finish that ties all the components together beautifully.

Step by Step Preparation

Preheat your oven to 400°F. On a baking sheet, toss the chopped zucchini, red and yellow bell peppers, and red onion with olive oil, salt, and pepper. Spread the vegetables in a single layer and roast in the oven for about 25-30 minutes, or until they are tender and the edges are slightly charred. Meanwhile, rinse the quinoa under cold water and drain. Bring the vegetable broth to a boil in a medium saucepan. Add the quinoa, reduce heat to low, cover, and simmer for 15 minutes or until the broth is absorbed and the quinoa is tender. Fluff the quinoa with a fork and let it cool slightly. In a large salad bowl, combine the roasted vegetables with the cooked quinoa. Add the crumbled feta cheese and drizzle with balsamic vinaigrette. Toss gently to combine. Serve the salad warm or at room temperature for the best flavor.

21. CAPRESE SANDWICH WITH PESTO

Servings:	Prep Time:
4	15 minutes

Ingredients:

- 8 slices of ciabatta bread
- 4 tablespoons pesto
- 2 large tomatoes sliced
- 1 ball fresh mozzarella sliced
- fresh basil leaves
- salt and pepper to taste
- balsamic glaze for drizzling.

About the Dish

The Caprese Sandwich with Pesto is a delightful celebration of simple, fresh ingredients. The classic combination of juicy tomatoes, creamy mozzarella, and vibrant basil is enhanced by the rich flavor of pesto, adding depth and a touch of garlic and pine nut. Drizzled with a sweet balsamic glaze, this sandwich is a gourmet take on traditional Italian flavors, packed into a crusty ciabatta that perfectly complements the soft fillings.

Step by Step Preparation

Begin by lightly toasting the ciabatta bread slices to add a bit of crunch and prevent them from becoming soggy once dressed. Spread a tablespoon of pesto on one side of each of four slices of bread. On these pesto-slathered slices, layer the fresh tomato slices and mozzarella slices. Season with salt and pepper, then add a few fresh basil leaves on top of the cheese. Drizzle with balsamic glaze for a touch of sweetness and acidity. Top with the remaining slices of bread. Press gently to adhere the components together. Cut each sandwich in half and serve immediately, enjoying the fresh burst of flavors that epitomize a perfect Caprese sandwich.

22. CARROT AND GINGER SOUP

Servings:	Prep Time:
4	35 minutes

Ingredients:

- 1 tablespoon olive oil
- 1 onion chopped

- 2 cloves garlic minced
- 4 cups chopped carrots
- 2 tablespoons grated fresh ginger
- 4 cups vegetable broth
- salt and pepper to taste
- 1 can coconut milk
- fresh cilantro for garnish.

About the Dish

Carrot and Ginger Soup is a smooth, velvety blend that warms from the inside out. The sweetness of the carrots is perfectly balanced by the zesty, spicy ginger, creating a comforting yet invigorating dish. This soup is enriched with creamy coconut milk, adding a luxurious texture and a subtle tropical flavor. It's not only a feast for the taste buds but also a boost for the immune system, thanks to the vitamins from the carrots and the anti-inflammatory properties of ginger.

Step by Step Preparation

Heat olive oil in a large pot over medium heat. Add chopped onion and minced garlic, sautéing until the onion is translucent and aromatic. Stir in the chopped carrots and grated ginger, cooking for a couple of minutes to meld the flavors. Pour in the vegetable broth, and season with salt and pepper. Bring to a boil, then reduce heat and simmer for about 25 minutes or until the carrots are very tender. Remove from heat and blend the soup using an immersion blender until completely smooth. Stir in the coconut milk until well combined, reheating gently if necessary. Serve the soup warm, garnished with fresh cilantro for an added layer of flavor and a pop of color.

23. LEMON BASIL ORZO WITH GRILLED VEGETABLES

Servings:
4

Prep Time:
30 minutes

Ingredients:

- 1 cup orzo pasta
- 2 zucchinis sliced
- 2 bell peppers (any color) sliced
- 1/2 cup cherry tomatoes halved
- 1/4 cup olive oil
- salt and pepper to taste
- juice and zest of 1 lemon
- 1/4 cup chopped fresh basil.

About the Dish

Lemon Basil Orzo with Grilled Vegetables is a light yet satisfying dish, perfect for those who appreciate bright, fresh flavors. The orzo is cooked until al dente and dressed with lemon juice and zest, providing a citrusy sharpness that is beautifully complemented by the sweet, smoky char of grilled vegetables. Fresh basil adds a fragrant, peppery touch that makes this dish a delightful summer meal or a perfect side to any protein.

Step by Step Preparation

Cook the orzo pasta according to package instructions until al dente, then drain and set aside to cool slightly. Meanwhile, brush the sliced zucchinis and bell peppers with olive oil and season with salt and pepper. Grill the vegetables on a preheated grill or grill pan until they have nice char marks and are tender, about 4-6 minutes per side. In a large mixing bowl, combine the cooked orzo with the grilled vegetables and cherry tomatoes. Drizzle with additional olive oil, lemon juice, and add the lemon zest. Toss to combine everything evenly. Stir in the chopped fresh basil just before serving. Season with additional salt and pepper if needed. Serve warm or at room temperature.

24. SPICY TOFU TACOS

Servings:
4

Prep Time:
25 minutes

Ingredients:

- 1 block firm tofu drained and crumbled
- 2 tablespoons olive oil
- 1 teaspoon chili powder
- 1/2 teaspoon cumin
- 1/2 teaspoon paprika
- salt and pepper to taste
- 8 corn tortillas
- 1 avocado sliced
- 1/4 cup chopped cilantro
- lime wedges for serving.

About the Dish

Spicy Tofu Tacos bring a plant-based flair to a beloved classic. Crumbled tofu, infused with a lively mix of chili powder, cumin, and paprika, offers a robust and smoky flavor that mimics the traditional taco filling but without the meat. This dish is not only vibrant and satisfying but also packs a protein punch that is both nutritious and heart-healthy. Fresh avocado adds a creamy texture that con-

trasts beautifully with the spice, and a sprinkle of cilantro introduces a burst of freshness that ties all the flavors together. Accompanied by a squeeze of lime, these tacos are a celebration of bold flavors and fresh ingredients, perfect for a quick dinner or a fun social gathering.

Step by Step Preparation

Heat the olive oil in a skillet over medium heat. Add the crumbled tofu to the skillet. Season with chili powder, cumin, paprika, salt, and pepper, mixing well to ensure the tofu is evenly coated with the spices. Cook the tofu for about 5-7 minutes, stirring occasionally, until it's golden and fragrant. This process not only cooks the tofu but allows it to absorb the flavors of the spices, enhancing its texture and taste.

While the tofu is cooking, prepare the tortillas. Heat them one at a time in a dry skillet or over an open flame, just until they become warm and slightly charred. Keep the tortillas warm by wrapping them in a clean kitchen towel as you prepare the rest.

To assemble the tacos, place an even amount of the spiced tofu mixture onto each warm tortilla. Top each taco with a few slices of avocado and a generous sprinkle of chopped cilantro. Serve the tacos with lime wedges on the side, encouraging diners to squeeze the lime over their tacos before enjoying them. The lime juice will add a bright, acidic contrast to the rich flavors of the taco filling. Serve immediately while the filling is warm and the tortillas are soft. These Spicy Tofu Tacos are perfect for a quick, flavorful meal that's sure to please both vegetarians and meat lovers alike with their fresh, bold flavors and satisfying textures.

25. SMOKED SALMON SALAD

Servings:
4

Prep Time:
15 minutes

Ingredients:

- 8 oz smoked salmon, thinly sliced
- 4 cups mixed greens (such as arugula and spinach)
- 1/2 red onion, thinly sliced
- 1 avocado, sliced
- 1/4 cup capers
- 2 tablespoons olive oil
- 1 tablespoon lemon juice
- salt and black pepper to taste
- fresh dill for garnish.

About the Dish

This Smoked Salmon Salad is an elegant yet easy-to-prepare dish that brings together the rich flavors of smoked salmon with the freshness of mixed greens and the creamy texture of avocado. The salty bite of capers and the sharpness of red onion complement the salmon perfectly, while a simple dressing of olive oil and lemon juice ties all the flavors together. Garnished with fresh dill, this salad is not only flavorful but also packed with omega-3 fatty acids, making it a heart-healthy choice.

Step by Step Preparation

Start by arranging the mixed greens on a large serving platter or in a salad bowl. Layer the thinly sliced smoked salmon over the greens. Add the sliced red onion and avocado on top of the salmon. Sprinkle capers across the salad for a burst of salty flavor. In a small bowl, whisk together the olive oil, lemon juice, salt, and black pepper to create a light dressing. Drizzle the dressing evenly over the salad. Garnish with fresh dill before serving to enhance the dish with a herby freshness. Serve immediately, enjoying the harmony of flavors and textures in this nutritious salad.

26. PUMPKIN AND COCONUT SOUP

Servings:
4

Prep Time:
45 minutes

Ingredients:

- 2 cups pumpkin puree
- 1 can coconut milk
- 1 onion, diced
- 2 cloves garlic, minced
- 1 tablespoon coconut oil
- 1 teaspoon curry powder
- 1/2 teaspoon ground ginger
- 4 cups vegetable broth
- salt and pepper to taste
- pumpkin seeds for garnish.

About the Dish

Pumpkin and Coconut Soup is a creamy, comforting dish with a hint of exotic flavors brought by curry and ginger. The sweetness of the pumpkin pairs wonderfully with the rich, creamy coconut milk, creating a velvety texture that's perfect for chilly evenings. This soup is not only a delight for the taste buds but also a nourishing option packed with vitamins and fiber.

Step by Step Preparation

In a large pot, heat the coconut oil over medium heat. Add the diced onion and minced garlic, sautéing until the onion is translucent. Stir in the curry powder and ground ginger, cooking for about a minute to release their flavors. Add the pumpkin puree and vegetable broth, stirring to combine. Bring the mixture to a boil, then reduce the heat and let it simmer for about 30 minutes to meld the flavors. Stir in the coconut milk and continue to simmer for another 10 minutes. Season with salt and pepper to taste. Use an immersion blender to puree the soup until smooth. Serve hot, garnished with pumpkin seeds for added crunch and visual appeal.

27. BEETROOT AND FETA SALAD

Servings:	Prep Time:
4	20 minutes

Ingredients:

- 3 medium beetroots, cooked and sliced
- 1/2 cup crumbled feta cheese
- 1/4 cup walnuts, toasted and chopped
- 2 cups arugula
- 1/4 red onion, thinly sliced
- 2 tablespoons olive oil
- 1 tablespoon balsamic vinegar
- salt and pepper to taste.

About the Dish

Beetroot and Feta Salad is a vibrant dish that combines the earthy sweetness of beetroots with the tangy sharpness of feta cheese. The toasted walnuts add a delightful crunch and nuttiness, while arugula provides a peppery backdrop. Dressed simply with olive oil and balsamic vinegar, this salad is a colorful, nutritious addition to any meal, offering a good balance of textures and flavors.

Step by Step Preparation

Arrange the arugula as the base of the salad in a large bowl or platter. Top with sliced cooked beetroots and thinly sliced red onion. Sprinkle crumbled feta cheese and toasted walnuts over the beets. In a small bowl, whisk together olive oil, balsamic vinegar, salt, and pepper to create a simple dressing. Drizzle the dressing over the salad just before serving to keep the arugula crisp. Toss gently to combine all the ingredients. This salad can be served immediately, offering a fresh, hearty accompaniment to any main course.

28. CHICKPEA AND SPINACH STEW

Servings:	Prep Time:
4	30 minutes

Ingredients:

- 1 can chickpeas, drained and rinsed
- 4 cups fresh spinach
- 1 onion, diced
- 2 cloves garlic, minced
- 2 tomatoes, diced
- 1 teaspoon cumin
- 1/2 teaspoon smoked paprika
- 2 tablespoons olive oil

- 4 cups vegetable broth
- salt and pepper to taste
- lemon wedges for serving.

About the Dish

Chickpea and Spinach Stew is a hearty, flavorful dish that combines nutrient-rich chickpeas with vibrant spinach in a savory broth infused with cumin and smoked paprika. This stew is a perfect choice for a filling meal that's both comforting and nutritious, providing plenty of protein, fiber, and essential vitamins.

Step by Step Preparation

Heat olive oil in a large pot over medium heat. Add diced onion and minced garlic, sautéing until the onion is soft and translucent. Stir in cumin and smoked paprika, cooking for another minute until the spices are fragrant. Add the diced tomatoes and cook for about 5 minutes, allowing them to break down and form a thick sauce. Add the drained chickpeas and vegetable broth, bringing the mixture to a simmer. Let it cook for about 15 minutes to allow the flavors to blend. Stir in the fresh spinach and cook until it is wilted, about 5 minutes. Season with salt and pepper to taste. Serve the stew hot, accompanied by lemon wedges for a bright, citrusy finish.

29. CAULIFLOWER TACOS WITH LIME CREMA

Servings:
4

Prep Time:
30 minutes

Ingredients:

- 1 head cauliflower, cut into small florets
- 2 tablespoons olive oil
- 1 teaspoon chili powder
- 1/2 teaspoon garlic powder
- 1/2 teaspoon cumin
- salt and pepper to taste
- 8 corn tortillas
- **for the lime crema:** 1/2 cup sour cream
- juice of 1 lime
- 1 tablespoon chopped cilantro
- additional cilantro for garnish.

About the Dish

Cauliflower Tacos with Lime Crema offer a delightful twist on traditional tacos, featuring roasted cauliflower as the star ingredient. Seasoned with chili powder, garlic, and cumin, the cauliflower florets develop a delicious, slightly crispy exterior that pairs beautifully with the zesty lime crema. This dish is a fantastic way to enjoy a meat-free meal without sacrificing flavor or satisfaction.

Step by Step Preparation

Preheat your oven to 400°F. Toss the cauliflower florets with olive oil, chili powder, garlic powder, cumin, salt, and pepper. Spread the florets on a baking sheet and roast in the oven for about 20-25 minutes, or until they are tender and golden with some crispy edges. While the cauliflower is roasting, prepare the lime crema by mixing sour cream, lime juice, and chopped cilantro in a small bowl. Set aside. Warm the corn tortillas in a skillet or directly over a flame just until they become pliable. To assemble the tacos, fill each tortilla with a generous amount of roasted cauliflower. Drizzle lime crema over the cauliflower, and garnish with additional cilantro. Serve immediately, enjoying the burst of flavors and textures in each bite.

30. PESTO CHICKEN SALAD WITH SPINACH

Servings:
4

Prep Time:
20 minutes

Ingredients:

- 2 cups cooked chicken breast, shredded
- 2 cups fresh spinach
- 1/4 cup prepared pesto
- 1/4 cup toasted pine nuts
- 1/2 cup cherry tomatoes, halved
- 1/4 cup shaved Parmesan cheese
- 2 tablespoons olive oil
- 1 tablespoon lemon juice
- salt and pepper to taste.

About the Dish

Pesto Chicken Salad with Spinach is a vibrant and flavorful dish that combines tender shredded chicken with the fresh, peppery taste of spinach, all dressed in a rich, herby pesto. The addition of toasted pine nuts provides a delightful crunch, while cherry tomatoes offer a juicy sweetness. Shaved Parmesan adds a final touch of salty, cheesy richness, making this salad both satisfying and gourmet.

Step by Step Preparation

In a large bowl, combine the shredded chicken and fresh spinach. Add the halved cherry tomatoes and toasted pine nuts. In a small bowl, whisk together the pesto, olive oil, and lemon juice to create a light dressing. Pour the dressing over the salad ingredients and toss gently to ensure everything is evenly coated. Season with salt and pepper to

taste. Sprinkle shaved Parmesan cheese over the top of the salad before serving. Serve this dish immediately to enjoy the fresh textures and bold flavors, perfect for a nutritious lunch or light dinner.

31. TURKEY AND QUINOA STUFFED PEPPERS

Servings:
4

Prep Time:
45 minutes

Ingredients:

- 4 bell peppers, halved and seeds removed
- 1 cup cooked quinoa
- 1 lb ground turkey
- 1 onion, diced
- 2 cloves garlic, minced
- 1 cup spinach, chopped
- 1 teaspoon paprika
- 1/2 teaspoon cumin
- 1 cup tomato sauce
- salt and pepper to taste
- 1/2 cup shredded mozzarella cheese.

About the Dish

Turkey and Quinoa Stuffed Peppers are a hearty, wholesome meal filled with a flavorful mix of ground turkey, quinoa, and spinach, seasoned with paprika and cumin. The bell peppers serve as an edible bowl, adding a sweet and crisp contrast to the savory filling. Topped with melted mozzarella, these stuffed peppers are not only nutritious but also visually appealing and comforting.

Step by Step Preparation

Preheat your oven to 375°F. In a skillet over medium heat, cook the ground turkey until it is browned. Add the diced onion and minced garlic, cooking until the onion is translucent. Stir in the chopped spinach, cooked quinoa, paprika, cumin, and tomato sauce. Season the mixture with salt and pepper, and cook until everything is well combined and the spinach is wilted. Spoon the turkey and quinoa mixture into each halved bell pepper, packing it tightly. Place the stuffed peppers in a baking dish and sprinkle shredded mozzarella cheese on top of each. Bake in the preheated oven for about 20-25 minutes, or until the peppers are tender and the cheese is bubbly and golden. Serve hot, offering a comforting and balanced meal.

32. ASIAN CHICKEN SALAD

Servings:
4

Prep Time:
20 minutes

Ingredients:

- 2 cups cooked chicken breast, shredded
- 3 cups mixed salad greens
- 1/2 cup shredded carrots
- 1/4 cup sliced almonds
- 1/2 red bell pepper, thinly sliced
- 1/4 cup crispy wonton strips
- **for the dressing:** 3 tablespoons soy sauce
- 2 tablespoons sesame oil
- 1 tablespoon honey
- 1 tablespoon rice vinegar
- 1 teaspoon grated ginger.

About the Dish

Asian Chicken Salad is a crisp, refreshing dish that blends tender shredded chicken with a medley of colorful vegetables and a tangy, sweet Asian-inspired dressing. The crispy wonton strips and sliced almonds add a delightful crunch that contrasts beautifully with the soft textures of the vegetables and chicken. This salad is perfect for a light lunch or as a side dish, providing a flavorful and visually stunning option.

Step by Step Preparation

In a large salad bowl, combine the shredded chicken, mixed salad greens, shredded carrots, thinly sliced red bell pepper, and sliced almonds. In a small bowl, whisk together soy sauce, sesame oil, honey, rice vinegar, and grated ginger to create the dressing. Drizzle the dressing over the salad and toss to coat evenly. Just before serving, sprinkle crispy wonton strips over the salad to maintain their crunch. Serve immediately, enjoying the burst of flavors and the mix of textures.

33. MOROCCAN COUSCOUS WITH ROASTED VEGETABLES

Servings:
4

Prep Time:
40 minutes

Ingredients:

- 1 cup couscous
- 2 cups vegetable broth
- 1 zucchini, cubed
- 1 red onion, chopped
- 1 bell pepper, cubed
- 1 carrot, sliced

- 2 tablespoons olive oil
- 1 teaspoon ground cumin
- 1/2 teaspoon cinnamon
- 1/4 cup raisins
- salt and pepper to taste
- fresh cilantro for garnish.

About the Dish

Moroccan Couscous with Roasted Vegetables is a colorful and aromatic dish that captures the essence of Moroccan cuisine. It features fluffy couscous, enhanced with a medley of spices like cumin and cinnamon, and is paired with a vibrant array of roasted vegetables. The addition of raisins offers a hint of sweetness that contrasts beautifully with the savory spices. Fresh cilantro adds a burst of flavor and color, rounding out this dish as a festive and nutritious meal.

Step by Step Preparation

Preheat your oven to 400°F. Toss the cubed zucchini, red onion, bell pepper, and sliced carrot with olive oil, ground cumin, cinnamon, salt, and pepper. Spread the vegetables on a baking sheet and roast in the oven for about 25-30 minutes, stirring occasionally, until they are tender and caramelized. Meanwhile, bring the vegetable broth to a boil in a medium saucepan. Add the couscous, cover, and remove from heat. Let it sit for 5 minutes, then fluff with a fork. Stir the roasted vegetables and raisins into the couscous. Adjust seasoning as needed. Garnish with freshly chopped cilantro before serving. This dish can be enjoyed hot or at room temperature, making it versatile for meal prep or immediate serving.

34. LENTIL AND MUSHROOM LOAF

Servings:	Prep Time:
6	1 hour

Ingredients:

- 1 cup dried lentils, cooked
- 1 cup finely chopped mushrooms
- 1 onion, finely chopped
- 2 cloves garlic, minced
- 1 cup breadcrumbs
- 1/2 cup grated Parmesan cheese
- 2 eggs, beaten
- 2 tablespoons tomato paste
- 1 teaspoon dried thyme
- salt and pepper to taste
- 1/4 cup ketchup for topping.

About the Dish

Lentil and Mushroom Loaf is a hearty, flavorful alternative to traditional meatloaf, perfect for those seeking a plant-based option. The lentils provide a firm texture and are a great source of protein, while the mushrooms add umami and richness. The combination of Parmesan cheese and herbs brings depth to the loaf, which is finished with a glaze of ketchup for a touch of sweetness.

Step by Step Preparation

Preheat your oven to 375°F and grease a loaf pan. In a large bowl, combine the cooked lentils, chopped mushrooms, onion, garlic, breadcrumbs, Parmesan cheese, beaten eggs, tomato paste, thyme, salt, and pepper. Mix well until everything is thoroughly combined. Press the mixture into the prepared loaf pan, smoothing the top with a spatula. Spread the ketchup evenly over the top. Bake in the preheated oven for about 40-45 minutes, or until the loaf is firm and the top is slightly caramelized. Let the loaf cool in the pan for 10 minutes before slicing. Serve warm with additional ketchup or your favorite sides.

35. ARTICHOKE AND SPINACH FLATBREAD

Servings:
4

Prep Time:
20 minutes

Ingredients:

- 2 pre-made flatbread crusts
- 1 cup canned artichoke hearts, drained and chopped
- 1 cup fresh spinach, chopped
- 1/2 cup ricotta cheese
- 1/4 cup mozzarella cheese, shredded
- 2 cloves garlic, minced
- 1 tablespoon olive oil
- salt and pepper to taste
- red pepper flakes for garnish.

About the Dish

Artichoke and Spinach Flatbread combines creamy, tangy artichoke hearts with the earthy taste of spinach atop a crispy flatbread crust. Ricotta and mozzarella cheeses add a creamy texture and a gooey melt, respectively, while garlic and olive oil infuse the flatbread with a robust flavor. This dish is perfect as an appetizer, light lunch, or part of a larger meal, offering a satisfying blend of flavors and textures.

Step by Step Preparation

Preheat your oven to 400°F. Brush each flatbread crust with olive oil and sprinkle minced garlic over them. Spread ricotta cheese on each crust as the base layer. Top with chopped artichoke hearts and fresh spinach. Sprinkle shredded mozzarella cheese over the top. Season with salt, pepper, and red pepper flakes for a bit of heat. Bake in the preheated oven for about 10-12 minutes, or until the edges are golden and the cheese is bubbly. Serve immediately, garnished with additional red pepper flakes if desired.

Chapter 3

Snacks

 ## INTRODUCTION TO HEALTHY SNACKING

Snacking is often perceived negatively, associated with mindless eating, unhealthy choices, and unnecessary calories. However, with a mindful and intentional approach, snacking can become a beneficial and integral part of a healthy eating pattern. In the **Living Good Daily Cookbook**, the "Healthy Snacking" section is designed to transform your snacking habits from potential dietary pitfalls into nourishing opportunities that support your health and well-being throughout the day.

The core of healthy snacking lies in choosing snacks that provide nutritional value and sustain your energy levels between meals. This involves more than just reaching for a piece of fruit or a handful of nuts, though these are excellent choices. It means thinking creatively about what a snack can be. The recipes in this section are crafted to offer a balance of macronutrients: proteins, fats, and carbohydrates in forms that are both wholesome and enjoyable. These aren't just fillers but purposeful mini-meals that help manage hunger, stabilize blood sugar levels, and prevent overeating at meal times.

Healthy snacking also extends beyond the foods you eat; it's about understanding your body's cues and responding appropriately. It requires recognizing the difference between true hunger and other triggers such as boredom or stress eating. This section of the cookbook provides insights into developing strategies for mindful eating, encouraging you to consider why you are eating and what your body actually needs at that moment.

Furthermore, this section includes a variety of recipes that are designed to satisfy different taste preferences and nutritional needs. From savory options like roasted chickpeas or turkey lettuce wraps to sweet treats like oatmeal energy balls or yogurt parfaits, each recipe is an opportunity to enjoy delicious flavors while nourishing your body. These snacks are quick to prepare, easy to pack, and perfect for on-the-go lifestyles, ensuring that you can always have a healthy option at hand.

In addition to providing tasty recipes, the "Healthy Snacking" section emphasizes the importance of portion control. Proper serving sizes are crucial to enjoying snacks that contribute to a balanced diet without overindulgence. By learning to portion your snacks correctly, you can enjoy a variety of foods while keeping your calorie intake in check.

The section also explores the role of hydration in snacking. Often, feelings of hunger are actually signs of dehydration. Including hydrating snacks such as fresh fruits with high water content, smoothies, or vegetables like cucumbers and bell peppers can help maintain hydration levels throughout the day, complementing your regular water intake.

Ultimately, the "Healthy Snacking" section of the cookbook aims to educate and inspire you to make choices that align with a healthy lifestyle. It's about changing the narrative around snacking, transforming it from a dieting challenge into a daily practice of fueling your body efficiently and deliciously. With the right knowledge and recipes, healthy snacking can become an enjoyable part of your routine that actively contributes to your overall health and satisfaction.

36. BAKED KALE CHIPS

Servings:
4

Prep Time:
15 minutes

Ingredients:

- 1 large bunch of kale, washed and dried
- 1 tablespoon olive oil
- salt to taste.

About the Dish

Baked Kale Chips offer a light and nutritious alternative to traditional snack chips. Rich in vitamins and minerals, these chips are made by lightly coating kale leaves with olive oil and a sprinkle of salt, then baking them until crispy. This simple snack is perfect for those seeking a healthy, crunchy treat that satisfies the urge for something salty.

Step by Step Preparation

Preheat your oven to 350°F (175°C). Tear the kale leaves from their stems and rip them into bite-size pieces. In a large bowl, toss the kale with olive oil and a pinch of salt, ensuring each piece is lightly coated. Spread the kale in a single layer on a baking sheet lined with parchment paper, taking care not to overcrowd the pan. Bake for about 10-15 minutes, or until the edges are crisp and slightly browned but not burnt. Watch closely to avoid overcooking. Let the chips cool on the baking sheet to enhance their crispiness before serving.

37. CARROT AND CUCUMBER STICKS WITH ALMOND DIP

Servings:
4

Prep Time:
10 minutes

Ingredients:

- 2 large carrots, peeled and cut into sticks
- 2 cucumbers, cut into sticks
- 1/2 cup almond butter
- 1 tablespoon honey
- 1 tablespoon lemon juice
- a pinch of salt.

About the Dish

Carrot and Cucumber Sticks with Almond Dip is a refreshing and nourishing snack that combines the crisp textures of fresh carrots and cucumbers with a creamy almond butter dip. This snack is perfect for those looking for a satisfying, healthful option that provides both crunch and flavor.

Step by Step Preparation

To make the almond dip, combine almond butter, honey, lemon juice, and a pinch of salt in a small bowl. Mix until smooth, adjusting the consistency with a little water if it's too thick. Slice the carrots and cucumbers into sticks for dipping. Arrange the vegetables on a plate and serve with the almond dip. This dish is ideal for an afternoon snack or as a healthy appetizer.

38. ENERGY PROTEIN BALLS

Servings:
8

Prep Time:
20 minutes

Ingredients:

- 1 cup rolled oats
- 1/2 cup almond butter
- 1/4 cup honey
- 1/4 cup protein powder
- 1/2 cup dried cranberries
- 1/4 cup ground flaxseed.

About the Dish

Energy Protein Balls are a convenient and tasty snack that provides a good balance of protein, fiber, and natural sugars, making them ideal for a quick energy boost. These balls are packed with nutritious ingredients like oats, almond butter, and flaxseed, which support sustained energy and health.

Step by Step Preparation

In a large bowl, mix rolled oats, almond butter, honey, protein powder, dried cranberries, and ground flaxseed until well combined. The mixture should be sticky enough to hold together. Roll the mixture into balls about the size of a golf ball. Place the balls on a parchment-lined tray and refrigerate for at least an hour to firm up. Store in an airtight container in the refrigerator for up to a week, grabbing one whenever you need a quick, healthy snack.

39. SPICY ROASTED CHICKPEAS

Servings:
4

Prep Time:
30 minutes

Ingredients:

- 2 cups cooked chickpeas, drained and dried
- 1 tablespoon olive oil
- 1/2 teaspoon chili powder
- 1/2 teaspoon garlic powder
- salt to taste.

About the Dish

Spicy Roasted Chickpeas are a crispy, flavorful snack that's easy to make and packed with protein. Seasoned with chili and garlic powder, these chickpeas are roasted to perfection, offering a satisfying crunch that makes them a perfect snack or a crunchy addition to salads.

Step by Step Preparation

Preheat your oven to 400°F (200°C). Pat the chickpeas dry with paper towels, removing as much moisture as possible to help them crisp up in the oven. Toss the chickpeas with olive oil, chili powder, garlic powder, and salt in a bowl. Spread the chickpeas on a baking sheet in a single layer. Roast for 20-25 minutes, shaking the pan occasionally to ensure even cooking. The chickpeas are done when they are golden and crispy. Let them cool before serving to enhance their crunch.

40. FRUIT AND NUT YOGURT

Servings:
4

Prep Time:
10 minutes

Ingredients:

- 2 cups plain Greek yogurt
- 1/2 cup mixed berries (strawberries, blueberries, raspberries)
- 1/4 cup mixed nuts (almonds, walnuts, pecans), chopped
- 1 tablespoon honey
- a sprinkle of cinnamon.

About the Dish

Fruit and Nut Yogurt is a delightful combination of creamy Greek yogurt, fresh berries, and crunchy nuts, sweetened naturally with honey and a hint of cinnamon. This nutritious snack is perfect for a quick breakfast, a satisfying snack, or a healthy dessert.

Step by Step Preparation

In individual bowls, spoon the Greek yogurt. Top with a generous helping of mixed berries and chopped nuts. Drizzle honey over the top and sprinkle with cinnamon for added flavor. Stir gently to combine just before eating, or enjoy the layers of texture and flavor as they are. This snack is best enjoyed fresh to maintain the crispness of the nuts and the freshness of the berries.

Chapter 4
Dinners

 ## INTRODUCTION TO NOURISHING EVENINGS

Evening meals are more than just the last meal of the day; they are an essential moment to nourish your body, indulge your senses, and bring a sense of closure to the activities and demands of the day. In the Living Good Daily Cookbook, the "Nourishing Evenings" section focuses on transforming dinner into a meaningful and restorative experience. This chapter is designed to balance the importance of nutrition with the enjoyment of food, ensuring that every meal satisfies your hunger and contributes to your overall well-being. Dinner is often a time of connection, where families, friends, or individuals pause to reflect, relax, and share a meal together. The recipes in this section are crafted to bring people together with dishes that are both nourishing and delicious, offering variety and balance to suit diverse tastes and dietary needs.

The goal of the "Nourishing Evenings" section is to provide meals that meet your nutritional needs while also satisfying your taste buds. The recipes focus on the use of whole foods, incorporating fresh vegetables, lean proteins, whole grains, and healthy fats. This thoughtful approach ensures that each meal is not only filling but also rich in nutrients that are essential for promoting health and vitality. Proper evening meals help your body replenish the vitamins and minerals that are depleted during the day, support metabolic health, and enhance your immune system. These meals are also designed to provide sustained energy, aid in digestion, and prepare your body for restful sleep. By focusing on these core aspects of health, the recipes in this section encourage a balanced and holistic approach to dinner, one that nurtures the body while delighting the palate.

Evening meals are also the perfect opportunity to practice mindful eating, which involves being fully present during your meal and savoring each bite. This practice can help you better understand your body's hunger and fullness cues, preventing overeating and promoting better digestion. The "Nourishing Evenings" section encourages you to slow down, appreciate the flavors and textures of your food, and truly enjoy the experience of eating. Mindful eating transforms dinner from a hurried routine into a deliberate and fulfilling ritual, offering physical and emotional nourishment. Each recipe is designed to inspire this sense of mindfulness, helping you cultivate a deeper appreciation for the food you prepare and consume.

In a fast-paced world, dinner is often rushed or reduced to convenience foods that do not provide the nourishment your body needs. The "Nourishing Evenings" section invites you to rethink this approach by making dinner a time to slow down, reconnect, and recharge. Preparing and enjoying a nourishing evening meal is not only an act of self-care but also an opportunity to foster connections with loved ones. It is a time to sit down together, share stories, and savor a meal that has been prepared with intention and care. The recipes in this section are designed to create moments of connection, whether you are enjoying a quiet dinner for one, preparing a meal for your family, or hosting a gathering with friends.

The importance of evening meals extends beyond the immediate pleasure of eating. Dinner provides the final opportunity of the day to fuel your body and prepare it for the restorative processes that occur during sleep. The food you eat in the evening impacts your energy levels, metabolism, and overall health. By choosing meals that are nutrient-dense and thoughtfully prepared, you can promote better digestion, improve sleep quality, and support your body's natural ability to repair and rejuvenate itself overnight. These recipes are designed to maximize these benefits by incorporating ingredients that provide a balance of protein, fiber, healthy fats, and essential vitamins and minerals.

The meals in this section are as diverse as they are nourishing, offering options for every palate and preference. From quick and simple dishes that are perfect for busy weeknights to more elaborate recipes that lend themselves to leisurely weekend cooking, the "Nourishing Evenings" section has something for everyone. Each recipe is crafted to be both flavorful and adaptable, allowing you to customize ingredients to suit your dietary needs or the ingredients you have on hand. The focus on whole, fresh ingredients ensures that every dish is bursting with flavor while supporting your health and well-being.

By emphasizing the use of seasonal and locally sourced produce, this section also encourages you to connect with the rhythms of nature and your local food community. Seasonal ingredients not only taste better but are also at their nutritional peak, offering the maximum health benefits. This connection to the seasons can add an extra layer of enjoyment and meaning to your meals, transforming dinner into an experience that nourishes both the body and the soul. Cooking with seasonal ingredients also allows for creativity in the kitchen, as you experiment with flavors and textures that reflect the time of year.

41. GRILLED SALMON WITH MANGO SALSA

Servings:	Prep Time:	Cook Time:
4	20 minutes	10 minutes

Ingredients:

- 4 salmon fillets (6 oz each)
- 1 tablespoon olive oil
- salt and pepper to taste
- 1 tablespoon lemon juice
- 1 ripe mango (peeled and diced)
- 1/4 cup red onion (finely diced)
- 1/4 cup fresh cilantro (chopped)
- 1 tablespoon lime juice
- 1 small jalapeno (seeded and minced, optional)
- salt and pepper to taste.

About the Dish:

Grilled Salmon with Mango Salsa is a flavorful and refreshing dish that combines the richness of grilled salmon with the sweet and tangy notes of fresh mango salsa. The salmon is grilled until perfectly flaky and moist, while the mango salsa brings a vibrant burst of flavor. The slight heat from the jalapeno and the acidity of the lime juice complement the sweetness of the mango, making this dish perfect for a summer meal or a light dinner.

Step by Step Preparation:

Preheat your grill or grill pan to medium-high heat. Brush the salmon fillets with olive oil and season with salt, pepper, and lemon juice. Place the salmon on the grill, skin-side down if applicable, and cook for 4-5 minutes per side, or until the salmon is cooked through and easily flakes with a fork. While the salmon is grilling, prepare the mango salsa by combining the diced mango, red onion, cilantro, lime juice, and jalapeno in a bowl. Season with salt and pepper to taste. Once the salmon is ready, remove it from the grill and serve with the mango salsa on top. This dish pairs wonderfully with a side of quinoa, rice, or steamed vegetables.

42. TURMERIC CHICKEN WITH COCONUT VEGGIE STIR FRY

Servings:	Prep Time:	Cook Time:
4	25 minutes	20 minutes

Ingredients:

- 4 boneless, skinless chicken breasts (cut into bite-sized pieces)
- 1 tablespoon turmeric powder
- 1 teaspoon ground cumin
- salt and pepper to taste
- 2 tablespoons olive oil
- 1 red bell pepper (sliced),
- 1 zucchini (sliced)
- 1 cup broccoli florets
- 1 cup carrots (julienned)
- 1 can (14 oz) coconut milk
- 2 cloves garlic (minced)
- 1 tablespoon fresh ginger (minced)
- 1 tablespoon soy sauce or coconut aminos
- fresh cilantro for garnish.

About the Dish:

Turmeric Chicken with Coconut Veggie Stir Fry is a vibrant and nourishing dish that brings together the warm, earthy flavors of turmeric with the creaminess of coconut milk. The chicken is seasoned with turmeric and cumin, giving it a rich flavor that complements the fresh vegetables. The coconut milk creates a smooth, velvety sauce that binds everything together, making each bite comforting and satisfying. This dish is not only packed with flavor but also with nutrients, as turmeric is known for its anti-inflammatory properties.

Step by Step Preparation:

Heat 1 tablespoon of olive oil in a large skillet over medium heat. Add the chicken pieces and season with salt, pepper, turmeric, and cumin. Cook for about 7-8 minutes, or until the chicken is golden brown and cooked through. Remove the chicken from the skillet and set it aside. In the same skillet, add the remaining tablespoon of olive oil and sauté the garlic and ginger for about 1 minute until fragrant. Add the red bell pepper, zucchini, broccoli, and carrots, and cook for 5-7 minutes, or until the vegetables are tender. Pour in the coconut milk and soy sauce, stirring to combine. Add the chicken back into the skillet and cook for an additional 2-3 minutes, ensuring everything is well-coated with the coconut sauce. Garnish with fresh cilantro and serve over rice or quinoa.

43. BLACK BEAN AND SWEET POTATO CHILI

Servings:
6

Prep Time:
15 minutes

Cook Time:
40 minutes

Ingredients:

- 2 medium sweet potatoes (peeled and diced)
- 1 tablespoon olive oil
- 1 onion (diced)
- 3 cloves garlic (minced)
- 1 teaspoon chili powder
- 1/2 teaspoon ground cumin
- 1/2 teaspoon smoked paprika
- salt and pepper to taste
- 2 cans (15 oz each) black beans (rinsed and drained)
- 1 can (14.5 oz) diced tomatoes
- 1 cup vegetable broth
- 1 tablespoon lime juice
- 1/4 cup fresh cilantro (chopped).

About the Dish:

Black Bean and Sweet Potato Chili is a hearty and flavorful vegetarian chili that combines the sweetness of roasted sweet potatoes with the savory, spiced flavors of black beans and tomatoes. The dish is packed with protein and fiber, making it both filling and nutritious. The chili powder and cumin provide warmth, while the smoked paprika adds a smoky depth to the dish. This chili is a great option for a cozy dinner or as a meal prep for the week.

Step by Step Preparation:

Preheat your oven to 400°F (200°C). Spread the diced sweet potatoes on a baking sheet and toss them with olive oil, salt, and pepper. Roast for about 20-25 minutes, or until the sweet potatoes are tender and lightly browned. While the sweet potatoes are roasting, heat 1 tablespoon of olive oil in a large pot over medium heat. Add the diced onion and cook for 5-7 minutes until softened. Add the minced garlic, chili powder, cumin, and smoked paprika, and cook for another minute until fragrant. Stir in the black beans, diced tomatoes, vegetable broth, and lime juice. Bring the mixture to a simmer and cook for 10-15 minutes to allow the flavors to meld together. Once the sweet potatoes are done, stir them into the chili. Let the chili simmer for another 5-10 minutes, then garnish with fresh cilantro before serving. This chili pairs well with a dollop of sour cream or a side of cornbread.

44. STUFFED BELL PEPPERS

Servings:	Prep Time:	Cook Time:
4	15 minutes	30 minutes

Ingredients:

- 4 bell peppers (any color)
- 1 cup cooked quinoa
- 1 can (15 oz) black beans (rinsed and drained)
- 1 cup corn kernels (fresh or frozen)
- 1/2 cup diced tomatoes
- 1 teaspoon cumin
- 1 teaspoon chili powder
- salt and pepper to taste
- 1/4 cup shredded cheese (optional)
- fresh cilantro for garnish.

About the Dish:

Stuffed Bell Peppers are a colorful and healthy dish that combines savory fillings of quinoa, black beans, corn, and tomatoes, all wrapped in tender bell peppers. These stuffed peppers are satisfying and nutrient-dense, providing fiber, protein, and a variety of vitamins. The seasoning of cumin and chili powder adds a warm, comforting flavor, and the optional shredded cheese adds a creamy fin-

ish. This dish can be served as a standalone meal or as a side to complement any protein.

Step by Step Preparation:

Preheat your oven to 375°F (190°C). Cut the tops off the bell peppers and remove the seeds and membranes. Place the peppers in a baking dish. In a bowl, mix together the cooked quinoa, black beans, corn, diced tomatoes, cumin, chili powder, salt, and pepper. Spoon the mixture into each bell pepper until they are full. If using, sprinkle shredded cheese on top of each stuffed pepper. Cover the baking dish with foil and bake for 25-30 minutes, or until the peppers are tender. Garnish with fresh cilantro before serving. These stuffed peppers are perfect for a hearty dinner or can be made in advance for meal prepping.

45. MUSHROOM AND SPINACH PASTA

Servings:	Prep Time:	Cook Time:
4	10 minutes	20 minutes

Ingredients:

- For this dish, you will need 8 oz pasta (spaghetti or fettuccine works well)
- 2 tablespoons olive oil
- 2 cloves garlic (minced)
- 8 oz mushrooms (sliced)
- 3 cups fresh spinach (washed)
- 1/2 cup vegetable broth
- 1/4 cup heavy cream
- salt and pepper to taste
- 1/4 cup grated Parmesan cheese.

About the Dish:

Mushroom and Spinach Pasta is a quick, easy, and nourishing dish that combines earthy mushrooms and fresh spinach with a creamy sauce. The vegetables are sautéed in olive oil with garlic, creating a savory base for the pasta. The richness of the cream and the slight saltiness of the Parmesan elevate the dish, while the mushrooms and spinach provide texture and nutrients. This dish is ideal for a weeknight dinner that's comforting but not overly heavy, offering a great balance of flavors.

Step by Step Preparation:

Start by cooking the pasta according to package directions. While the pasta is cooking, heat the olive oil in a large pan over medium heat. Add the minced garlic and sauté for about 1 minute, or until fragrant. Add the sliced mushrooms to the pan and cook for 5-7 minutes, or until they are browned and tender. Stir in the fresh spinach and cook until wilted, about 2-3 minutes. Add the vegetable broth and bring to a simmer. Once the broth has reduced slightly, stir in the heavy cream and cook for another 2 minutes. Season with salt and pepper to taste. Once the pasta is done, drain it and add it to the pan with the mushroom and spinach mixture. Toss everything together, allowing the pasta to soak up the sauce. Serve with grated Parmesan cheese on top.

46. BAKED TILAPIA WITH LEMON HERB SAUCE

Servings:
4

Prep Time:
10 minutes

Cook Time:
15 minutes

Ingredients:

- For this dish, you will need 4 tilapia fillets (about 6 oz each)
- 2 tablespoons olive oil, salt and pepper to taste
- 2 tablespoons fresh parsley (chopped)
- 1 tablespoon fresh dill (chopped)
- 1 tablespoon lemon zest
- 2 tablespoons lemon juice
- 1 teaspoon garlic powder
- 1 teaspoon onion powder.

About the Dish:

Baked Tilapia with Lemon Herb Sauce is a light, flavorful dish that features the delicate taste of tilapia paired with a fresh, citrusy sauce. The tilapia is baked to tender perfection, while the lemon and herb sauce adds a burst of flavor that brings out the best in the fish. This dish is quick to prepare, making it perfect for a healthy dinner any night of the week. The combination of lemon, parsley, and dill offers a refreshing and fragrant sauce that complements the mild flavor of the tilapia.

Step by Step Preparation:

Preheat your oven to 375°F (190°C). Place the tilapia fillets on a baking sheet lined with parchment paper and drizzle with olive oil. Season with salt, pepper, garlic powder, and onion powder. Bake the tilapia for about 12-15 minutes, or until the fish is opaque and easily flakes with a fork. While the fish is baking, combine the lemon zest, lemon juice, parsley, and dill in a small bowl to make the lemon herb sauce. Once the tilapia is cooked, remove it from the oven and drizzle the lemon herb sauce over the top of each fillet. Serve immediately with a side of roasted vegetables or a simple salad for a complete meal.

47. VEGAN MUSHROOM STROGANOFF

Servings:	Prep Time:	Cook Time:
4	15 minutes	25 minutes

Ingredients:

- For this dish, you will need 8 oz wide egg noodles or gluten-free pasta
- 2 tablespoons olive oil
- 1 onion (diced)
- 3 cloves garlic (minced)
- 10 oz mushrooms (sliced)
- 1 tablespoon flour (use a gluten-free variety if needed)
- 1 cup vegetable broth
- 1/2 cup unsweetened coconut milk
- 1 tablespoon soy sauce or coconut aminos
- salt and pepper to taste
- fresh parsley for garnish.

About the Dish:

Vegan Mushroom Stroganoff is a dairy-free and hearty version of the classic stroganoff. This dish is filled with savory mushrooms, a creamy coconut milk sauce, and a subtle richness from the soy sauce. The egg noodles or pasta provide a comforting base, and the flavor profile is deep and earthy. It's a satisfying meal for anyone following a vegan diet, yet it's so full of flavor that even non-vegans will enjoy it. This dish is perfect for a cozy evening when you're craving comfort food with a plant-based twist.

Step by Step Preparation:

Cook the pasta according to the package instructions. While the pasta is cooking, heat the olive oil in a large pan over medium heat. Add the diced onion and sauté for 3-4 minutes until softened. Add the minced garlic and sliced mushrooms and cook for 5-7 minutes until the mushrooms have released their moisture and are nicely browned. Sprinkle the flour over the mushrooms and stir to coat, cooking for 1-2 minutes. Slowly pour in the vegetable broth, stirring constantly to avoid lumps. Add the coconut milk and soy sauce, and bring the mixture to a simmer. Cook for another 5-7 minutes until the sauce thickens to your desired consistency. Season with salt and pepper to taste. Drain the pasta and add it to the pan with the mushroom sauce, tossing to coat the noodles evenly. Garnish with fresh parsley before serving.

48. THAI GREEN CURRY WITH TOFU

Servings:	Prep Time:	Cook Time:
4	20 minutes	25 minutes

Ingredients:

- For this dish, you will need 14 oz firm tofu (pressed and cubed)
- 1 tablespoon sesame oil
- 1 onion (sliced)
- 2 cloves garlic (minced)
- 1 tablespoon ginger (minced)
- 2 tablespoons Thai green curry paste
- 1 can (14 oz) coconut milk
- 1 cup vegetable broth

- 1 red bell pepper (sliced)
- 1 zucchini (sliced)
- 1 cup broccoli florets
- 2 tablespoons soy sauce or coconut aminos
- 1 tablespoon lime juice
- fresh cilantro for garnish.

About the Dish:

Thai Green Curry with Tofu is a vibrant and fragrant dish packed with fresh vegetables and silky tofu. The green curry paste gives the dish its signature spice and flavor, while the coconut milk creates a creamy base that perfectly complements the vegetables. This dish is a warm, comforting choice and works wonderfully with jasmine rice or rice noodles for a satisfying meal. The tofu adds protein and absorbs the delicious flavors of the curry, making it both filling and nutritious.

Step by Step Preparation:

Heat sesame oil in a large pot over medium heat. Add the sliced onion, minced garlic, and ginger, and sauté for 3-4 minutes until the onion is softened. Stir in the green curry paste and cook for 1-2 minutes, allowing the spices to release their fragrance. Add the coconut milk and vegetable broth, and bring to a simmer. Once the curry is simmering, add the cubed tofu, red bell pepper, zucchini, and broccoli, and cook for 10-15 minutes until the vegetables are tender and the tofu is heated through. Stir in the soy sauce and lime juice, adjusting the seasoning to taste. Serve the curry over jasmine rice or noodles, and garnish with fresh cilantro before serving.

49. BEEF AND BROCCOLI STIR-FRY

Servings:	**Prep Time:**	**Cook Time:**
4	15 minutes	20 minutes

Ingredients:

- You will need 1 pound of beef sirloin or flank steak, sliced thinly against the grain
- For the stir-fry sauce, use 2 tablespoons soy sauce or coconut aminos
- 1 tablespoon sesame oil
- 1 tablespoon olive oil
- 3 cloves of garlic minced
- 1 tablespoon fresh ginger minced
- 4 cups broccoli florets
- 1/4 cup beef broth
- 1 tablespoon honey, 1 tablespoon rice vinegar
- 2 teaspoons cornstarch, and 1 tablespoon water. For garnish, add sesame seeds.

About the Dish:

Beef and Broccoli Stir-Fry is a quick and flavorful dish, perfect for busy weeknights when you're craving something satisfying but healthy. The tender beef slices are paired with crisp broccoli in a savory sauce made with soy sauce, honey, and rice vinegar. The stir-fry technique preserves the crunch of the broccoli while allowing the beef to soak up the rich, umami flavors of the sauce. It's a hearty, protein-packed dish that's also loaded with nutrients from the broccoli, making it both filling and nourishing.

Step by Step Preparation:

Start by slicing the beef thinly against the grain and marinating it in 2 tablespoons of soy sauce for about 10-15 minutes. While the beef marinates, heat 1 tablespoon of sesame oil and 1 tablespoon of olive oil in a large skillet or wok over medium-high heat. Add the minced garlic and ginger and sauté for about 1 minute until fragrant. Add the beef to the skillet and cook for about 4-5 minutes, or until browned and cooked through. Remove the beef from the skillet and set it aside. In the same skillet, add the broccoli florets and sauté for 4-5 minutes, adding a little more oil if necessary. In a small bowl, combine the beef broth, honey, rice vinegar, and cornstarch mixed with water. Pour this sauce over the broccoli and bring it to a simmer for 2-3 minutes, allowing the sauce to thicken. Add the beef back into the skillet and stir everything together until well coated. Garnish with sesame seeds and serve over steamed rice or noodles.

50. SPAGHETTI SQUASH WITH TOMATO BASIL SAUCE

Servings:	Prep Time:	Cook Time:
4	15 minutes	40 minutes

Ingredients:

- You will need 1 medium spaghetti squash
- 2 tablespoons olive oil
- salt and pepper to taste
- 1 can (14 oz) crushed tomatoes
- 2 cloves garlic minced
- 1 teaspoon dried oregano
- 1/4 teaspoon red pepper flakes (optional)
- 1/4 cup fresh basil chopped
- 1/4 cup Parmesan cheese (optional).

About the Dish:

Spaghetti Squash with Tomato Basil Sauce is a light, low-carb alternative to traditional pasta dishes. The spaghetti squash, when roasted, turns into tender, noodle-like strands that provide a satisfying base for the rich, tangy tomato sauce. The sauce is made from fresh tomatoes, garlic, basil, and a hint of red pepper flakes, creating a balance of flavors that complement the squash perfectly. This dish is ideal for anyone looking for a healthier twist on a classic Italian favorite.

Step by Step Preparation:

Preheat your oven to 400°F (200°C). Cut the spaghetti squash in half lengthwise and remove the seeds. Drizzle the inside of each half with olive oil and season with salt and pepper. Place the squash halves face down on a baking sheet and roast for about 35-40 minutes, or until the flesh is tender and can be easily scraped into strands with a fork. While the squash is roasting, prepare the tomato basil sauce. Heat the olive oil in a saucepan over medium heat and add the minced garlic. Sauté for 1-2 minutes until fragrant, then add the crushed tomatoes, oregano, and red pepper flakes. Simmer for 15-20 minutes, allowing the sauce to thicken. Once the squash is done, use a fork to scrape the flesh into spaghetti-like strands. Serve the spaghetti squash in bowls, topped with the tomato basil sauce and garnished with fresh basil and Parmesan cheese if desired.

51. VEGETABLE AND CHICKPEA CURRY

Servings:	Prep Time:	Cook Time:
4	20 minutes	30 minutes

Ingredients:

- For this dish, you will need 1 tablespoon olive oil
- 1 onion diced
- 2 cloves garlic minced
- 1 tablespoon grated fresh ginger
- 2 teaspoons curry powder
- 1 teaspoon cumin
- 1/2 teaspoon turmeric
- salt to taste
- 1 can (15 oz) chickpeas rinsed and drained
- 1 medium sweet potato peeled and diced
- 1 zucchini diced
- 1 red bell pepper diced
- 1 can (14 oz) diced tomatoes
- 1 can (14 oz) coconut milk
- 1 cup vegetable broth
- 1 tablespoon lime juice
- 1/4 cup fresh cilantro chopped.

About the Dish:

Vegetable and Chickpea Curry is a hearty, flavorful, and nourishing dish that's packed with vegetables and protein-rich chickpeas. The curry spices, including turmeric, cumin, and curry powder, infuse the dish with warmth and complexity, while the coconut milk provides a creamy base that helps bring everything together. The sweet potatoes and zucchini add a touch of sweetness and texture, making this curry filling and well-balanced. This dish is a great option for a cozy dinner or as a meal prep for the week.

Step by Step Preparation:

Heat the olive oil in a large pot over medium heat. Add the diced onion and sauté for 5-7 minutes until softened. Add the minced garlic, ginger, curry powder, cumin, turmeric, and salt, and cook for another minute until fragrant. Stir in the chickpeas, diced sweet potato, zucchini, and red bell pepper, and cook for another 5 minutes. Pour in the diced tomatoes, coconut milk, and vegetable broth, and bring to a simmer. Let the curry cook for 20-25 minutes, or until the vegetables are tender. Once the vegetables are cooked, stir in the lime juice and fresh cilantro. Serve the curry hot, paired with rice or naan for a complete meal.

52. KOREAN BIBIMBAP

Servings:	Prep Time:	Cook Time:
4	25 minutes	15 minutes

Ingredients:

- For this dish, you will need 2 cups cooked rice
- 1 tablespoon sesame oil
- 1/2 pound ground beef or tofu (for a vegetarian version)
- 1 tablespoon soy sauce
- 1 teaspoon garlic powder
- 1/4 teaspoon black pepper
- 1 cup spinach blanched
- 1/2 cup shredded carrots
- 1/2 cucumber julienned

- 2 eggs, 1 tablespoon gochujang (Korean chili paste)
- 1 teaspoon sesame seeds
- fresh cilantro for garnish.

About the Dish:

Korean Bibimbap is a vibrant and flavorful dish that combines various sautéed vegetables, rice, protein, and a fried egg, all topped with a spicy gochujang sauce. The word "bibimbap" literally means "mixed rice," and that's exactly how this dish is enjoyed—everything is mixed together before eating. The combination of textures, from crunchy vegetables to tender rice, and the richness of the fried egg makes this dish both satisfying and nutritious. Bibimbap is an ideal meal for those looking for a balance of flavors and nutrients.

Step by Step Preparation:

Start by cooking your rice according to package instructions. While the rice is cooking, heat sesame oil in a skillet over medium-high heat. Add the ground beef or tofu and cook until browned, seasoning with soy sauce, garlic powder, and black pepper. While the beef or tofu is cooking, blanch the spinach and sauté the carrots and cucumber in separate pans until just tender. Fry the eggs sunny-side up. To assemble, divide the cooked rice into bowls and top with the beef or tofu, sautéed vegetables, a fried egg, and a spoonful of gochujang. Garnish with sesame seeds and fresh cilantro before serving.

53. CAULIFLOWER STEAK WITH HERB SAUCE

Servings:	Prep Time:	Cook Time:
4	15 minutes	25 minutes

Ingredients:

- You will need 1 large cauliflower, cut into 4 thick slices
- 2 tablespoons olive oil
- salt and pepper to taste
- 1 tablespoon fresh thyme (chopped)
- 1 tablespoon fresh rosemary (chopped)
- 2 tablespoons lemon juice
- 1/4 cup fresh parsley (chopped)
- 1 garlic clove (minced), and 1 tablespoon Dijon mustard.

About the Dish:

Cauliflower Steak with Herb Sauce is a beautifully simple yet flavorful dish that transforms the humble cauliflower into a hearty, satisfying main course. The cauliflower steaks are roasted to perfection with a golden, crispy exterior and a tender inside. Topped with a vibrant herb sauce made from fresh rosemary, thyme, parsley, garlic, and Dijon mustard, this dish offers a burst of fresh flavors and a perfect balance of textures. It's an ideal choice for those seeking a plant-based, low-carb alternative to traditional meat dishes.

Step by Step Preparation:

Preheat your oven to 400°F (200°C). Remove the leaves from the cauliflower and carefully slice it into 1-inch thick "steaks." Drizzle the cauliflower steaks with olive oil and season with salt, pepper, and fresh thyme and rosemary. Place the steaks on a baking sheet and roast in the oven for 20-25 minutes, flipping halfway through, until the cauliflower is golden brown and tender. While the cauliflower roasts, prepare the herb sauce by mixing the lemon juice, parsley, garlic, Dijon mustard, and a little olive oil in a small bowl. Once the cauliflower is ready, plate the steaks and drizzle them generously with the herb sauce before serving. This dish pairs beautifully with quinoa, rice, or a light salad.

54. JERK CHICKEN WITH MANGO SALSA

Servings:	Prep Time:	Cook Time:
4	15 minutes	25 minutes

Ingredients:

- For the chicken, you will need 4 bone-in, skin-on chicken thighs
- 2 tablespoons olive oil
- 2 tablespoons jerk seasoning
- salt and pepper to taste.
- For the mango salsa, use 1 ripe mango (peeled and diced)
- 1/4 cup red onion (finely diced)
- 1/4 cup cilantro (chopped)
- 1 tablespoon lime juice
- 1 small jalapeno (minced, optional), and salt and pepper to taste.

About the Dish:

Jerk Chicken with Mango Salsa combines the spicy, flavorful kick of traditional Jamaican jerk chicken with the sweetness of fresh mango salsa. The chicken is marinated in a rich blend of spices, then grilled or roasted to crispy perfection. The mango salsa, made with juicy, ripe mango, adds a refreshing and tropical element to the dish, balancing the heat from the jerk seasoning. This dish is perfect for a summer meal or any time you're craving bold flavors.

Step by Step Preparation:

Preheat your grill or oven to medium-high heat. Rub the chicken thighs with olive oil and season them generously with jerk seasoning, salt, and pepper. If grilling, cook the chicken for 5-7 minutes per side, or until the internal temperature reaches 165°F (74°C). If baking, roast the chicken in the oven at 375°F (190°C) for 25-30 minutes. While the chicken is cooking, prepare the mango salsa by combining the diced mango, red onion, cilantro, lime juice, and jalapeno in a bowl. Season with salt and pepper to taste. Once the chicken is cooked, remove it from the grill or oven and let it rest for a few minutes. Serve the jerk chicken with a generous spoonful of mango salsa on top. This dish pairs wonderfully with rice, roasted vegetables, or a simple salad.

55. ZUCCHINI LASAGNA

Servings:	Prep Time:	Cook Time:
4	20 minutes	40 minutes

Ingredients:

- You will need 4 medium zucchinis (sliced into thin strips lengthwise)
- 2 tablespoons olive oil
- 1 onion (diced)
- 2 cloves garlic (minced)

- 1 can (14 oz) crushed tomatoes
- 1 tablespoon tomato paste
- 1 teaspoon dried oregano
- 1/4 teaspoon red pepper flakes (optional)
- 1 cup ricotta cheese
- 1/4 cup fresh basil (chopped)
- 2 cups shredded mozzarella cheese, salt and pepper to taste.

About the Dish:

Zucchini Lasagna is a lighter, healthier version of traditional lasagna that uses zucchini slices in place of pasta sheets. The zucchini is thinly sliced and layered with a rich, savory tomato sauce, creamy ricotta, and melted mozzarella, creating a dish that's as comforting as it is nutritious. This recipe is a great option for those looking to cut carbs or incorporate more vegetables into their diet while still enjoying the flavors of a classic Italian dish.

Step by Step Preparation:

Preheat your oven to 375°F (190°C). Slice the zucchinis lengthwise into thin strips and lightly salt them to draw out excess moisture. Let them sit for 10 minutes, then pat dry with a paper towel. Heat olive oil in a pan over medium heat. Add the diced onion and garlic, cooking for 5 minutes until softened. Stir in the crushed tomatoes, tomato paste, oregano, red pepper flakes (if using), and salt and pepper. Simmer the sauce for 15-20 minutes, allowing the flavors to meld. In a small bowl, mix the ricotta cheese with fresh basil. To assemble, layer zucchini slices in a baking dish, followed by a layer of tomato sauce, a few spoonfuls of ricotta, and a sprinkle of mozzarella cheese. Repeat the layers until all ingredients are used, finishing with a layer of mozzarella on top. Bake for 25-30 minutes, or until the cheese is melted and bubbly. Let the lasagna rest for 5 minutes before serving. This dish pairs wonderfully with a side salad or garlic bread.

56. LAMB KOFTAS WITH TZATZIKI

Servings:	Prep Time:	Cook Time:
4	20 minutes	15 minutes

Ingredients:

- For the koftas, you will need 1 pound ground lamb
- 1 small onion (finely diced)
- 2 cloves garlic (minced)
- 1 tablespoon fresh parsley (chopped)
- 1 teaspoon ground cumin
- 1 teaspoon ground coriander
- 1/2 teaspoon cinnamon
- salt and pepper to taste
- For the tzatziki sauce, use 1 cup Greek yogurt
- 1 cucumber (grated)
- 1 tablespoon lemon juice
- 2 tablespoons fresh dill (chopped)
- 1 clove garlic (minced), and salt to taste.

About the Dish:

Lamb Koftas with Tzatziki are a flavorful, spiced dish that is perfect for grilling. The koftas, made from ground lamb, are seasoned with cumin, coriander, and cinnamon, giving them a warm, aromatic flavor. Paired with a refreshing, cool tzatziki sauce made from yogurt, cucumber, and dill, this dish is a great balance of savory and fresh. The tzatziki adds a creamy, tangy contrast to the spiced lamb, making it a perfect combination. This dish is perfect for a light dinner or served as part of a Mediterranean spread.

Step by Step Preparation:

In a large bowl, combine the ground lamb, onion, garlic, parsley, cumin, coriander, cinnamon, salt, and pepper. Mix everything together until well combined. Divide the mixture into 8 equal portions and roll them into balls, then shape them into elongated koftas. Heat a grill or grill pan over medium-high heat and cook the koftas for 4-5 minutes on each side, or until browned and cooked through. While the koftas are cooking, prepare the tzatziki sauce by combining the Greek yogurt, grated cucumber, lemon juice, dill, garlic, and salt in a bowl. Stir to combine. Once the koftas are ready, remove them from the grill and serve with a generous spoonful of tzatziki sauce on top. This dish pairs well with pita bread, a Greek salad, or roasted vegetables.

57. RATATOUILLE WITH POLENTA

Servings:	Prep Time:	Cook Time:
4	15 minutes	30 minutes

Ingredients:

- For the ratatouille, you will need 1 tablespoon olive oil
- 1 medium eggplant (diced)
- 1 zucchini (diced)
- 1 bell pepper (diced)
- 1 onion (diced)
- 2 cloves garlic (minced)
- 1 can (14.5 oz) diced tomatoes
- 1 teaspoon dried thyme
- 1/2 teaspoon dried oregano
- salt and pepper to taste.
- For the polenta, use 1 cup cornmeal
- 4 cups vegetable broth
- 1 tablespoon olive oil
- 1/2 cup grated Parmesan cheese (optional)
- salt and pepper to taste.

About the Dish:

Ratatouille with Polenta is a colorful, comforting dish that combines a hearty vegetable stew with creamy polenta. The ratatouille features tender, roasted vegetables simmered in a tomato-based sauce, bringing together the flavors of eggplant, zucchini, bell pepper, and onion. Served with a base of polenta, which adds a creamy texture and rich flavor, this dish is both satisfying and nourishing. The polenta complements the stewed vegetables perfectly, making it a great option for a cozy, vegetable-forward meal.

Step by Step Preparation:

Start by heating 1 tablespoon of olive oil in a large pan over medium heat. Add the diced eggplant, zucchini, bell pepper, and onion, and sauté for about 8-10 minutes, or until the vegetables are softened. Add the garlic and cook for an additional minute until fragrant. Stir in the diced tomatoes, thyme, oregano, salt, and pepper. Let the mixture simmer for 15-20 minutes, stirring occasionally, until the vegetables are tender and the sauce has thickened. While the ratatouille is cooking, prepare the polenta by bringing the vegetable broth to a boil in a medium saucepan. Slowly whisk in the cornmeal and cook, stirring constantly, for 5-7 minutes, or until the polenta has thickened. Once thick, stir in olive oil, Parmesan cheese (if using), salt, and pepper. To serve, spoon the polenta onto plates and top with the ratatouille. Garnish with fresh herbs and enjoy!

58. FISH AND PESTO PASTA

Servings:	Prep Time:	Cook Time:
4	10 minutes	20 minutes

Ingredients:

- For this dish, you will need 4 white fish fillets (such as cod, tilapia, or haddock)
- 8 oz pasta (spaghetti or penne works well)
- 2 tablespoons olive oil
- 1/4 cup pesto (store-bought or homemade)
- salt and pepper to taste
- 1 tablespoon lemon juice
- 1/4 cup Parmesan cheese (optional)
- fresh basil for garnish.

About the Dish:

Fish and Pesto Pasta is a deliciously light and flavorful dish that combines tender fish with aromatic pesto sauce and al dente pasta. The fish fillets are seared in olive oil, creating a crispy exterior while remaining flaky on the inside. The pesto, with its rich basil, garlic, and Parmesan flavors, adds a fresh and vibrant layer to the dish. This simple recipe is packed with healthy omega-3 fats from the fish, and the pasta provides the perfect base for the pesto to shine. This dish is both light and filling, making it a great weeknight dinner option.

Step by Step Preparation:

Begin by cooking the pasta according to the package instructions. While the pasta is cooking, heat the olive oil in a skillet over medium-high heat. Season the fish fillets with salt and pepper, then place them in the pan. Cook for 3-4 minutes on each side, or until the fish is golden brown and cooked through. Remove the fish from the pan and set it aside. In the same pan, add the pesto and heat it gently for a couple of minutes. Once the pasta is cooked, drain it and add it to the pan with the pesto. Toss the pasta to coat it evenly with the sauce. Serve the pesto pasta topped with the fish fillets, a drizzle of lemon juice, and a sprinkle of Parmesan cheese if desired. Garnish with fresh basil and serve with a side salad or steamed vegetables.

59. PORTOBELLO MUSHROOM BURGERS

Servings:	Prep Time:	Cook Time:
4	10 minutes	15 minutes

Ingredients:

- For this dish, you will need 4 large Portobello mushrooms (stems removed)
- 2 tablespoons olive oil
- salt and pepper to taste
- 1/2 teaspoon garlic powder
- 1/2 teaspoon onion powder
- 4 whole wheat burger buns
- 1/4 cup fresh basil (chopped)
- 1/2 cup shredded mozzarella cheese (optional)
- 1/4 cup balsamic vinegar
- 1 tablespoon honey
- 1 cup mixed greens
- 1 tomato (sliced), and 1 small red onion (sliced).

About the Dish:

Portobello Mushroom Burgers are a delicious vegetarian alternative to traditional beef burgers. The Portobello mushrooms are grilled or sautéed with garlic powder and onion powder, resulting in a savory, meaty texture that makes them the perfect substitute for a burger patty. The balsamic vinegar glaze adds a tangy sweetness, and the fresh basil and mozzarella cheese provide additional flavor and creaminess. This dish is both filling and nutritious, offering a healthy take on a classic comfort food.

Step by Step Preparation:

Preheat your grill or grill pan to medium-high heat. Brush the Portobello mushrooms with olive oil and season with salt, pepper, garlic powder, and onion powder. Grill the mushrooms for 5-6 minutes per side, or until they are tender and nicely charred. While the mushrooms are grilling, heat the balsamic vinegar and honey in a small saucepan over medium heat. Bring to a simmer and cook for 3-4 minutes, or until the glaze has thickened slightly. Once the mushrooms are cooked, remove them from the grill and drizzle the balsamic glaze over the top. Toast the burger buns lightly and assemble the burgers by placing a grilled mushroom cap on the bottom of each bun. Top with fresh basil, mozzarella (if using), tomato slices, red onion, and a handful of mixed greens. Place the top bun on the assembled burger and serve with your favorite sides.

60. CHICKEN TIKKA MASALA

Servings:	**Prep Time:**	**Cook Time:**
4	20 minutes	30 minutes

Ingredients:

- For the chicken, you will need 4 boneless, skinless chicken breasts (cut into cubes)
- 1 tablespoon garam masala
- 1 tablespoon ground cumin
- 1 tablespoon ground coriander
- 1 teaspoon turmeric
- salt and pepper to taste
- 2 tablespoons yogurt
- 2 tablespoons olive oil
- For the sauce, you will need 1 onion (diced)
- 3 cloves garlic (minced)
- 1 tablespoon grated ginger
- 1 can (14.5 oz) diced tomatoes
- 1/2 cup coconut milk
- 1/4 cup heavy cream
- 2 teaspoons ground cumin
- 1 teaspoon ground coriander
- 1/2 teaspoon cayenne pepper
- fresh cilantro for garnish.

About the Dish:

Chicken Tikka Masala is a rich, flavorful dish that features tender pieces of chicken marinated in a blend of spices, then cooked in a creamy, spiced tomato sauce. The spices, including garam masala, cumin, and coriander, create a complex and aromatic base, while the coconut milk and heavy cream make the sauce luxuriously smooth. This dish is perfect for those craving comforting, bold flavors and is often enjoyed with naan or rice to soak up the flavorful sauce.

Step by Step Preparation:

In a large bowl, combine the chicken cubes with garam masala, cumin, coriander, turmeric, salt, pepper, and yogurt. Mix well and marinate for at least 15 minutes. In a large pan, heat olive oil over medium heat and sauté the diced onion, garlic, and ginger until softened and fragrant, about 5 minutes. Stir in the diced tomatoes, coconut milk, heavy cream, cumin, coriander, and cayenne pepper, and simmer for 10 minutes to thicken the sauce. Add the marinated chicken to the sauce and cook for 10-15 minutes, or until the chicken is fully cooked through. Garnish with fresh cilantro and serve with basmati rice or naan for a complete meal.

Chapter 5

Desserts

 ## INTRODUCTION TO GUILT-FREE DESSERTS

Desserts have always been a source of joy, comfort, and indulgence. They are often the highlight of a meal, the sweet treat that signals the end of a wonderful gathering or a quiet moment of relaxation. But the problem with traditional desserts is that they often come with a sense of guilt. Loaded with sugar, refined flour, and unhealthy fats, they can leave us feeling sluggish and regretful. This is where guilt-free desserts come in, offering a healthier alternative that lets us enjoy our favorite sweets without compromising our well-being. These desserts are designed with wholesome, nutrient-rich ingredients that nourish the body while still satisfying that desire for something sweet. Instead of relying on refined sugars, guilt-free desserts use natural sweeteners like honey, maple syrup, or fruit to bring the sweetness we crave. They also incorporate ingredients like nuts, seeds, and whole grains, which provide essential nutrients and fiber to help keep us feeling full and satisfied. Guilt-free desserts are not just a healthier option, they are a way to redefine how we view desserts altogether. These treats allow us to indulge in the simple pleasure of sweetness without the aftermath of sugar crashes or the bloated feeling that often accompanies indulgent treats.

One of the most appealing aspects of guilt-free desserts is that they do not force us to choose between taste and nutrition. In fact, they show us that it is entirely possible to have both. These desserts are bursting with flavor, and the use of whole foods ensures that they are just as satisfying, if not more so, than traditional desserts. For example, a rich chocolate mousse made from avocado can provide healthy fats and antioxidants, while a fruit-based sorbet made from frozen berries can be both refreshing and naturally sweet. The beauty of guilt-free desserts is that they allow us to enjoy our favorite flavors without the guilt or heaviness that comes with eating too much sugar or processed ingredients. They let us feel good about what we are eating, and not just in the moment but in the long term as well. By using wholesome ingredients, guilt-free desserts can provide sustained energy and help balance blood sugar levels, so you don't experience the crash that typically follows a sugar-laden dessert. What makes these desserts even better is their ability to satisfy cravings in a way that is both nutritious and indulgent. Whether it's a creamy coconut milk-based pudding or a no-bake cheesecake made with cashews, guilt-free desserts are just as decadent, comforting, and flavorful as traditional options, and they leave us feeling nourished rather than sluggish.

Moreover, guilt-free desserts offer endless opportunities for creativity and experimentation. There are so many ways to combine different flavors and textures to create something exciting and new. From baked goods made with almond flour to energy balls packed with dried fruits and seeds, the options are endless. These desserts also allow you to explore alternative ingredients, such as coconut flour or date paste, that may not only provide a healthier alternative but also bring new textures and flavors into your kitchen. With guilt-free desserts, you can create treats that are as satisfying as the ones you grew up with but without the processed ingredients that often leave you feeling less than great. In the pages ahead, you will find that guilt-free desserts are not just for those on special diets or health-conscious eaters. They are for anyone who loves dessert and wants to enjoy it without the negative consequences. These recipes are designed to be enjoyed by all, whether you are looking to cut back on sugar, incorporate more whole foods into your diet, or simply enjoy the pleasures of dessert in a healthier way.

Desserts hold a unique place in our lives. They are the treats we crave when celebrating, comforting us after a tough day, or simply satisfying that desire for something sweet. Yet, for many, these indulgences come with a sense of guilt. The sugar, flour, and unhealthy fats commonly found in traditional desserts can leave us feeling sluggish and, in some cases, regretting our choices. But what if you could enjoy dessert without that guilt? What if you could indulge in something sweet and still feel good about it? This is the magic of guilt-free desserts. They allow us to savor the sweetness we love, but without the negative aftermath. These desserts focus on using wholesome, natural ingredients that nourish the body while still satisfying the palate. They incorporate natural sweeteners like honey, maple syrup, or fruit, and often feature whole foods like nuts, seeds, and plant-based ingredients. This shift not only makes these desserts a healthier option but also opens up a world of new flavors and textures.

Unlike traditional sweets that may leave you feeling lethargic after consumption, guilt-free desserts offer lasting energy. By using ingredients such as oats, chia seeds, coconut flour, and almond meal, they provide fiber and protein that help stabilize blood sugar levels. No more sugar crashes or feelings of regret after indulging in these treats. They satisfy your cravings while fueling your body with nutrients. These desserts are not just for those with dietary restrictions, although they are often gluten-free, dairy-free, or vegan-friendly. They are for anyone who loves dessert but wants to feel better after eating it. Guilt-free desserts invite you to explore new ways of preparing sweets that not only taste great but also support your wellness goals. With these desserts, it's no longer about choosing between indulgence and health; you can have both.

The great thing about guilt-free desserts is their versatility. You can create a wide variety of treats that cater to all tastes and preferences. From rich, creamy treats made with avocados or coconut milk, to fruit-based desserts that are naturally sweetened, the possibilities are endless. You might be surprised at how delicious and satisfying these alternatives can be. A raw chocolate truffle made from dates and cocoa, for example, can provide the same rich chocolatey satisfaction as a traditional truffle, but with the added benefits of fiber and antioxidants. Or consider a smoothie bowl topped with fresh fruit and nuts, giving you the sweetness and texture of a traditional dessert but with added nutritional value. These desserts offer a refreshing twist on familiar favorites, making it easier to enjoy indulgence without the guilt.

Creating guilt-free desserts is not only about making healthy choices. It is also about discovering new ingredients and flavors that you might not have used before. Perhaps you've never baked with almond flour or coconut flour, but both are excellent alternatives to traditional flour, offering a rich texture and healthy fats. You might not have considered using avocados in desserts, but they make for the creamiest, most decadent bases for puddings and mousses. These new ingredients provide fresh opportunities to experiment in the kitchen, and with each new creation, you can feel good about nourishing your body with wholesome ingredients.

As you dive into the world of guilt-free desserts, you'll realize just how easy and enjoyable it is to make healthy alternatives to your favorite treats. Whether you are preparing a batch of energy bites to snack on throughout the week, baking a light and fluffy almond flour cake, or blending up a refreshing fruit sorbet, you'll find that these desserts are just as indulgent as their traditional counterparts. The key difference is that guilt-free desserts are made with ingredients that support your body's health, allowing you to enjoy them fully without feeling weighed down or regretful afterward.

61. RAW CHOCOLATE AVOCADO MOUSSE

Servings:
4

Prep Time:
10 minutes

Ingredients:

- For this dish, you will need 2 ripe avocados
- 1/4 cup raw cacao powder
- 1/4 cup maple syrup or honey
- 1 teaspoon vanilla extract
- 1/4 cup almond milk (or any plant-based milk), and a pinch of salt.

About the Dish:

Raw Chocolate Avocado Mousse is a rich and creamy dessert that combines the healthy fats of avocado with the deep flavor of raw cacao. The avocados create a velvety texture, making this mousse both satisfying and smooth. The sweetness from maple syrup or honey enhances the chocolate flavor, while the almond milk adds the perfect touch of creaminess. Not only does this dessert taste indulgent, but it also provides nourishing ingredients that are good for you. The raw cacao offers antioxidants, while the avocados provide healthy fats, making this mousse a guilt-free treat for any occasion.

Step by Step Preparation:

Start by scooping the flesh of the avocados into a food processor or blender. Add the raw cacao powder, maple syrup or honey, vanilla extract, and almond milk. Blend until smooth and creamy, scraping down the sides as needed to ensure everything is well incorporated. Taste and adjust the sweetness if necessary. Once the mousse reaches a smooth, mousse-like consistency, spoon it into serving dishes. Chill for at least 30 minutes in the refrigerator before serving. Top with a few berries or a sprinkle of cacao nibs for an extra touch of flavor.

62. BAKED APPLES WITH HONEY AND NUTS

Servings:
4

Prep Time:
10 minutes

Cook Time:
20 minutes

Ingredients:

- 4 apples (such as Gala or Fuji)
- 1/4 cup chopped walnuts or almonds
- 2 tablespoons honey
- 1/2 teaspoon cinnamon
- 1 tablespoon coconut oil, and a pinch of salt.

About the Dish:

Baked Apples with Honey and Nuts is a warm, comforting dessert that brings out the natural sweetness of apples. The apples are cored and filled with a mixture of nuts, honey, and cinnamon, then baked to perfection. As they bake, the apples become tender and caramelized, making each bite a deliciously sweet and satisfying treat. The nuts add a satisfying crunch, while the honey and cinnamon enhance the overall flavor. This dessert is perfect for a cozy evening or as a light, naturally sweet treat after dinner.

Step by Step Preparation:

Preheat your oven to 350°F (175°C). Core the apples, leaving the bottom intact to create a hollow space for the filling. In a small bowl, combine the chopped walnuts or almonds, honey, cinnamon, and a pinch of salt. Stuff each apple with the nut mixture, pressing it gently to ensure it fits snugly inside. Place the apples in a baking dish and drizzle them with melted coconut oil. Bake for 20-25 minutes, or until the apples are tender and slightly caramelized. Serve warm, topped with a drizzle of honey or a scoop of dairy-free ice cream for an extra treat.

63. COCONUT FLOUR LEMON BARS

Servings:	Prep Time:	Cook Time:
8	15 minutes	25 minutes

Ingredients:

- For the crust, you will need 1 cup coconut flour
- 1/4 cup melted coconut oil
- 2 tablespoons honey
- 1/4 teaspoon salt, and 1 egg
- For the filling, you will need 3 eggs
- 1/2 cup honey
- 1/2 cup freshly squeezed lemon juice
- 1 tablespoon lemon zest, and 1/4 cup coconut flour.

About the Dish:

Coconut Flour Lemon Bars are a refreshing dessert that offers the perfect balance of sweet and tangy flavors. The coconut flour crust provides a light, nutty base, while the lemon filling brings a zesty and citrusy punch that is both refreshing and satisfying. These bars are gluten-free, naturally sweetened, and made with wholesome ingredients. The combination of coconut flour and lemon makes for a light yet indulgent treat, perfect for anyone looking to enjoy a healthier dessert without sacrificing flavor.

Step by Step Preparation:

Preheat your oven to 350°F (175°C). In a bowl, combine the coconut flour, melted coconut oil, honey, salt, and egg. Mix well until a dough forms. Press the dough into the bottom of a greased 8x8-inch baking pan, ensuring it's evenly spread. Bake the crust for 10-12 minutes, or until lightly golden brown. While the crust is baking, prepare the filling by whisking together the eggs, honey, lemon juice, lemon zest, and coconut flour. Once the crust is done, pour the filling over the hot crust and return the pan to the oven. Bake for an additional 15-18 minutes, or until the filling is set and lightly golden on top. Allow the bars to cool completely before cutting into squares. Serve chilled or at room temperature for a refreshing treat.

64. DARK CHOCOLATE COVERED STRAWBERRIES

Servings:	Prep Time:	Cook Time:
6	10 minutes	5 minutes

Ingredients:

- You will need 12 fresh strawberries (washed and dried thoroughly)
- 4 oz dark chocolate (70% cocoa or higher)
- 1 tablespoon coconut oil, and sea salt for garnish (optional).

About the Dish:

Dark Chocolate Covered Strawberries are a simple yet indulgent treat that combines the sweetness of ripe strawberries with the richness of dark chocolate. The smooth, velvety chocolate coating creates a perfect balance with the juicy, fresh strawberries. Dark chocolate not only adds depth and intensity to the flavor but also provides antioxidants and health benefits. This dessert is a delightful option for anyone craving a sweet, satisfying treat that is both light and rich at the same time. The addition of sea salt can take these strawberries to the next level by adding a hint of savory contrast to the sweet and bitter flavors of the chocolate.

Step by Step Preparation:

Start by washing the strawberries and patting them dry with a paper towel to ensure there's no excess moisture. Place the strawberries on a piece of parchment paper or a baking sheet lined with wax paper. In a small saucepan, melt the dark chocolate and coconut oil together over low heat, stirring occasionally until smooth. Once the chocolate is fully melted and well combined, remove it from the heat. Holding each strawberry by the stem, dip it into the melted chocolate, making sure to coat about two-thirds of the strawberry. Allow any excess chocolate to drip off before placing the dipped strawberry on the parchment paper. If desired, sprinkle a tiny pinch of sea salt over each dipped strawberry for added flavor. Let the strawberries set at room temperature for about 5 minutes or place them in the refrigerator for 15 minutes to harden the chocolate. Serve the chocolate-covered strawberries as an elegant dessert for a dinner party, or enjoy them as a sweet snack any time.

65. ALMOND JOY ENERGY BALLS

Servings:
12

Prep Time:
15 minutes

Ingredients:

- You will need 1 cup almond butter
- 1/2 cup unsweetened shredded coconut
- 1/4 cup honey or maple syrup
- 1/4 cup ground flaxseed
- 1/4 cup dark chocolate chips
- 1/2 teaspoon vanilla extract, and a pinch of salt.

About the Dish:

Almond Joy Energy Balls are a healthier, bite-sized version of the classic candy bar, offering a satisfying combination of sweet, salty, and nutty flavors. These energy balls are packed with protein, fiber, and healthy fats, making them an ideal snack or quick dessert. The almond butter gives them a creamy texture, while the shredded coconut adds a chewy element, and the dark chocolate chips offer a hint of indulgence. These energy balls are naturally sweetened with honey or maple syrup, providing just the right amount of sweetness without the added sugars found in many store-bought snacks. These bites are not only perfect for a midday pick-me-up, but they are also great as a post-workout snack to fuel your body.

Step by Step Preparation:

In a large bowl, combine the almond butter, shredded coconut, honey or maple syrup, ground flaxseed, vanilla extract, and a pinch of salt. Stir the mixture well until everything is evenly combined.

Add the dark chocolate chips and mix them into the dough. Once the mixture is ready, roll it into small balls, about 1 inch in diameter, and place them on a baking sheet or plate lined with parchment paper. Once all the balls are shaped, place them in the refrigerator for at least 30 minutes to firm up. These energy balls can be stored in an airtight container in the fridge for up to a week, making them a convenient and healthy snack to have on hand whenever you need a quick energy boost.

66. CARROT CAKE BITES

Servings:
12

Prep Time:
10 minutes

Ingredients:

- You will need 1 cup shredded carrots
- 1/2 cup rolled oats
- 1/4 cup almond flour
- 1/4 cup unsweetened shredded coconut
- 1/4 cup raisins
- 1/4 cup walnuts (chopped)
- 1 tablespoon maple syrup
- 1/2 teaspoon cinnamon, and a pinch of salt.

About the Dish:

Carrot Cake Bites are a portable, healthier take on the classic carrot cake, packed into bite-sized portions that are perfect for satisfying sweet cravings. These little bites are full of flavor and texture, thanks to the carrots, raisins, walnuts, and a touch of cinnamon. The use of oats and almond flour creates a light and wholesome base that adds fiber and protein, making these bites a great option for a post-workout snack or a mid-afternoon treat.

With the combination of natural sweetness from the carrots and maple syrup, along with the satisfying crunch of walnuts and raisins, these carrot cake bites deliver all the beloved flavors of carrot cake in a much healthier and more convenient form.

Step by Step Preparation:

In a large bowl, combine the shredded carrots, rolled oats, almond flour, shredded coconut, raisins, chopped walnuts, cinnamon, and a pinch of salt. Add the maple syrup and mix everything together until it's evenly incorporated. If the mixture feels too dry, add a little more maple syrup or a splash of water to help bind it together. Roll the mixture into small balls, about 1 inch in diameter, and place them on a baking sheet or plate lined with parchment paper. Once all the bites are shaped, refrigerate them for at least 30 minutes to allow them to firm up. These carrot cake bites can be stored in the fridge for up to a week, making them a convenient and healthy snack to keep on hand. Enjoy them as a quick treat or pair them with your favorite nut butter for an extra boost.

67. VEGAN RASPBERRY CHEESECAKE

Servings:
6

Prep Time:
15 minutes

Chill Time:
4 hours

Ingredients:

- For the crust, you will need 1 cup almonds
- 1/2 cup pitted dates
- 2 tablespoons coconut oil, and a pinch of salt.
- For the filling, use 1 1/2 cups raw cashews (soaked for at least 4 hours)

- 1/4 cup coconut oil (melted)
- 1/4 cup maple syrup
- 1 teaspoon vanilla extract
- 1/2 cup fresh raspberries, and 1 tablespoon lemon juice.

About the Dish:

Vegan Raspberry Cheesecake is a decadent, creamy dessert that tastes just like the real thing but without any dairy or refined sugar. The crust is made from wholesome almonds and dates, creating a satisfying base that holds together beautifully. The filling is rich and velvety, thanks to soaked cashews blended with coconut oil and maple syrup. The raspberries give the cheesecake a fresh, tart flavor that perfectly complements the creamy filling. This dessert is perfect for those who follow a plant-based lifestyle but still want to indulge in something luxurious and sweet. It's also gluten-free, making it an excellent option for those with dietary restrictions.

Step by Step Preparation:

Start by preparing the crust. In a food processor, blend the almonds, pitted dates, coconut oil, and a pinch of salt until the mixture becomes sticky and crumbly. Press the mixture into the bottom of a springform pan or a pie dish to form an even crust. Place it in the freezer to set while you prepare the filling. In a high-speed blender, combine the soaked cashews, melted coconut oil, maple syrup, vanilla extract, raspberries, and lemon juice. Blend until smooth and creamy, scraping down the sides as needed. Once the filling is ready, pour it over the chilled crust and spread it evenly. Place the cheesecake in the refrigerator for at least 4 hours, or until it has firmed up. Once chilled, slice and serve with fresh raspberries on top for an added burst of flavor. Enjoy this refreshing and indulgent dessert as a guilt-free treat.

68. PEACH AND BLUEBERRY CRISP

Servings:	Prep Time:	Cook Time:
6	10 minutes	30 minutes

Ingredients:

- For the filling, you will need 2 cups fresh peaches (diced)
- 1 cup fresh blueberries
- 2 tablespoons maple syrup
- 1 tablespoon lemon juice
- 1 teaspoon cinnamon, and 1 tablespoon cornstarch.
- For the topping, use 1/2 cup rolled oats
- 1/4 cup almond flour
- 1/4 cup coconut sugar
- 1/4 teaspoon cinnamon
- 2 tablespoons coconut oil (melted), and a pinch of salt.

About the Dish:

Peach and Blueberry Crisp is a warm, comforting dessert that brings together the natural sweetness of peaches and blueberries, with a crunchy, lightly sweetened topping. This crisp is perfect for showcasing the flavors of fresh, seasonal fruit, and it offers a healthier alternative to traditional fruit crisps that are often loaded with sugar. The combination of juicy peaches, blueberries, and a hint of cinnamon creates a deliciously fragrant filling, while the topping made from oats and almond flour gives the dish the perfect amount of texture. It's a wholesome dessert that is both satisfying and light, making it perfect for a family gathering or a weeknight treat.

Step by Step Preparation:

Preheat your oven to 375°F (190°C). In a bowl, combine the diced peaches, blueberries, maple syrup, lemon juice, cinnamon, and cornstarch. Stir everything together until the fruit is well-coated, then transfer the mixture into a baking dish. In a separate bowl, mix together the oats, almond flour, coconut sugar, cinnamon, melted coconut oil, and a pinch of salt. Stir until everything is well combined and the mixture forms a crumbly texture. Sprinkle the oat topping evenly over the fruit mixture. Bake for 25-30 minutes, or until the top is golden brown and the fruit is bubbling. Let the crisp cool for a few minutes before serving. It's perfect on its own or topped with a scoop of dairy-free vanilla ice cream for a more indulgent treat.

69. NO-BAKE PEANUT BUTTER BARS

Servings:	**Prep Time:**	**Chill Time:**
12	10 minutes	1 hour

Ingredients:

- 1 cup peanut butter (preferably natural, unsweetened)
- 1/4 cup maple syrup
- 1/2 cup rolled oats
- 1/4 cup coconut flour
- 1/4 teaspoon vanilla extract
- a pinch of salt, and 1/4 cup dark chocolate chips.

About the Dish:

No-Bake Peanut Butter Bars are a quick, easy, and delicious treat that comes together in just a few minutes. These bars are rich and satisfying, thanks to the creamy peanut butter and the natural sweetness from maple syrup. The addition of rolled oats and coconut flour gives the bars a chewy texture that's both hearty and filling. Topped with a layer of dark chocolate, these peanut butter bars are the perfect balance of sweet and salty. Whether you're looking for a post-workout snack, a quick dessert, or a midday energy boost, these bars are an excellent option. Best of all, they require no baking and can be made ahead of time for a convenient treat whenever you need it.

Step by Step Preparation:

In a medium bowl, combine the peanut butter, maple syrup, rolled oats, coconut flour, vanilla extract, and a pinch of salt. Stir well until everything is thoroughly mixed and the mixture becomes thick and sticky. Press the mixture into the bottom of a parchment-lined baking dish, spreading it out evenly. Melt the dark chocolate chips in the microwave or over a double boiler, then drizzle the melted chocolate over the peanut butter mixture. Use a spatula to spread the chocolate evenly over the bars. Place the baking dish in the refrigerator for at least 1 hour to allow the bars to firm up. Once chilled, cut the bars into squares and enjoy. These no-bake peanut butter bars can be stored in an airtight container in the fridge for up to a week.

70. CHIA PUDDING WITH ALMOND MILK

Servings:
4

Prep Time:
5 minutes

Chill Time:
4 hours

Ingredients:

1/2 cup chia seeds, 2 cups almond milk (or any plant-based milk), 2 tablespoons maple syrup, 1 teaspoon vanilla extract, and a pinch of salt. Optional toppings include fresh berries, shredded coconut, or nuts.

About the Dish:

Chia Pudding with Almond Milk is a simple, nourishing dessert that's packed with healthy omega-3 fatty acids, fiber, and protein. This dessert is not only incredibly easy to make but also customizable, allowing you to experiment with different flavors and toppings. The chia seeds absorb the almond milk, creating a thick, pudding-like texture that is both creamy and satisfying. Sweetened with maple syrup and enhanced with a hint of vanilla, this pudding is naturally sweet and full of flavor. It's perfect as a light dessert, a breakfast, or a snack, and it can be prepared in advance for busy days.

Step by Step Preparation:

In a bowl, combine the chia seeds, almond milk, maple syrup, vanilla extract, and a pinch of salt. Stir everything together until the chia seeds are evenly distributed. Let the mixture sit for 5 minutes, then stir again to ensure that the seeds don't clump together. Cover the bowl and place it in the refrigerator for at least 4 hours, or overnight, to allow the chia seeds to absorb the liquid and thicken. Once the pudding has set, give it a good stir and top with your favorite toppings, such as fresh berries, shredded coconut, or chopped nuts. Serve chilled for a refreshing and healthy dessert.

71. MANGO COCONUT POPSICLES

Servings:
6

Prep Time:
10 minutes

Freeze Time:
4 hours

Ingredients:

- You will need 2 ripe mangoes (peeled and diced)
- 1/2 cup canned coconut milk (full-fat)
- 2 tablespoons honey or maple syrup
- 1/2 teaspoon vanilla extract, and a pinch of salt.

About the Dish:

Mango Coconut Popsicles are a refreshing and tropical treat that's perfect for hot weather. The sweet and tangy mangoes pair beautifully with the creamy coconut milk, creating a smooth and satisfying popsicle. This dessert is not only delicious but also packed with vitamins and healthy fats, making it a guilt-free indulgence. The combination of mango's natural sweetness and the richness of coconut makes these popsicles a refreshing yet satisfying option for a snack or dessert. With just a few simple ingredients, these popsicles come together quickly and can be enjoyed by everyone, whether you're cooling off after a workout or treating yourself to something special.

Step by Step Preparation:

Start by blending the mangoes, coconut milk, honey or maple syrup, vanilla extract, and a pinch of salt in a blender or food processor until smooth. Pour the mixture into popsicle molds, ensuring that each mold is filled evenly. If you don't have popsicle molds, you can also use small plastic cups or ice cube trays. Insert sticks into the molds and freeze for at least 4 hours, or until completely frozen. Once the popsicles are set, remove them from the molds and enjoy immediately. For an extra touch, you can dip the popsicles in melted dark chocolate or sprinkle with toasted coconut flakes before freezing for an added layer of flavor.

72. ALMOND COCONUT FUDGE BITES

Servings:	Prep Time:	Cook Time:
12	10 minutes	30 minutes

Ingredients:

- You will need 1 cup almond butter
- 1/2 cup shredded unsweetened coconut
- 2 tablespoons maple syrup
- 1/4 cup coconut oil (melted)
- 1/4 cup cocoa powder
- 1 teaspoon vanilla extract, and a pinch of sea salt.

About the Dish:

Almond Coconut Fudge Bites are rich, decadent, and packed with wholesome ingredients. The almond butter provides a creamy base, while the shredded coconut adds a chewy texture, making these bites both satisfying and indulgent. The addition of cocoa powder gives them a rich chocolatey flavor that pairs perfectly with the natural sweetness of maple syrup. These bites are naturally sweetened and are a great option for anyone looking for a healthier alternative to traditional fudge. They come together quickly and are perfect for a snack, dessert, or even a post-workout treat. With just a few ingredients, these fudge bites are a simple, delicious, and nutrient-dense indulgence.

Step by Step Preparation:

In a mixing bowl, combine the almond butter, shredded coconut, maple syrup, melted coconut oil, cocoa powder, vanilla extract, and a pinch of sea salt. Stir until all ingredients are fully incorporated and the mixture becomes smooth. Line a baking sheet or tray with parchment paper and spoon the mixture into small bite-sized portions, rolling them into balls. Place the balls on the baking sheet and refrigerate for at least 30 minutes to allow them to firm up. Once chilled, enjoy these bite-sized treats as a sweet snack or a healthy dessert. Store any leftovers in an airtight container in the fridge for up to a week.

73. AVOCADO CHOCOLATE CHIP COOKIES

Servings:	Prep Time:	Cook Time:
12	15 minutes	12 minutes

Ingredients:

- You will need 1 ripe avocado (mashed)
- 1/4 cup coconut sugar
- 1/4 cup maple syrup

- 1 teaspoon vanilla extract
- 1 egg, 1 cup almond flour
- 1/2 teaspoon baking soda
- 1/4 teaspoon salt, and 1/2 cup dairy-free chocolate chips.

About the Dish:

Avocado Chocolate Chip Cookies are a healthier twist on the classic chocolate chip cookie, replacing butter with creamy avocado for a rich, soft texture. The avocado adds healthy fats and makes the cookies moist, while the coconut sugar and maple syrup provide natural sweetness. These cookies are gluten-free and dairy-free, yet they taste just as delicious as traditional chocolate chip cookies. The combination of almond flour and chocolate chips ensures a satisfying treat that's both indulgent and nourishing. Whether you're enjoying them as a snack or serving them at a gathering, these cookies are sure to impress while being kind to your body.

Step by Step Preparation:

Preheat your oven to 350°F (175°C). In a large mixing bowl, mash the ripe avocado until smooth. Add the coconut sugar, maple syrup, vanilla extract, and egg to the mashed avocado and mix well until fully combined. In a separate bowl, whisk together the almond flour, baking soda, and salt. Gradually add the dry ingredients to the wet ingredients, mixing until the dough comes together. Fold in the chocolate chips. Line a baking sheet with parchment paper and drop spoonfuls of dough onto the sheet, spacing them about 2 inches apart. Bake for 10-12 minutes, or until the edges of the cookies are golden brown. Allow the cookies to cool on the baking sheet for a few minutes before transferring them to a wire rack to cool completely.

74. BLUEBERRY LEMON CHEESECAKE BARS

Servings: 8	**Prep Time:** 20 minutes	**Cook Time:** 30 minutes

Ingredients:

For the crust, you will need 1 cup almond flour, 1/4 cup shredded coconut, 2 tablespoons melted coconut oil, and 1 tablespoon maple syrup. For the filling, use 2 cups raw cashews (soaked for at least 4 hours), 1/2 cup coconut milk, 1/4 cup maple syrup, 2 tablespoons lemon juice, 1 teaspoon lemon zest, and 1/2 cup fresh blueberries.

About the Dish:

Blueberry Lemon Cheesecake Bars are a fresh and tangy dessert that combines the creaminess of cashew-based "cheesecake" with the sweet, tart flavors of blueberries and lemon. The crust made from almond flour and shredded coconut adds a crunchy base that contrasts nicely with the creamy, velvety filling. The blueberries add a burst of natural sweetness and a pop of color, making these bars as beautiful as they are delicious. These bars are dairy-free, gluten-free, and refined-sugar-free, making them an excellent choice for anyone looking to enjoy a healthier dessert that doesn't sacrifice taste.

Step by Step Preparation:

Preheat your oven to 350°F (175°C). For the crust, mix the almond flour, shredded coconut, melted coconut oil, and maple syrup in a bowl until fully combined. Press the mixture into the bottom of a lined 8x8-inch baking pan and bake for 10-12 minutes, or until lightly golden. While the crust is baking, prepare the filling by blending the soaked cashews, coconut milk, maple syrup, lemon juice, and lemon zest in a high-speed blender until smooth and creamy. Pour the filling over the baked crust and smooth the top with a spatula. Drop spoonfuls of fresh blueberries on top of the filling and gently swirl them in with a toothpick or knife. Bake for an additional 20-25 minutes, or until the edges are set and the center is slightly firm. Let the bars cool to room temperature before refrigerating them for at least 2 hours to firm up. Slice into bars and serve chilled.

75. PISTACHIO AND DATE TRUFFLES

Servings:	Prep Time:	Chill Time:
12	10 minutes	30 minutes

Ingredients:

- 1 cup unsalted pistachios (shelled)
- 1 cup pitted dates
- 1/4 cup shredded coconut
- 2 tablespoons almond butter
- 1/2 teaspoon vanilla extract, and a pinch of sea salt.

About the Dish:

Pistachio and Date Truffles are a simple, wholesome treat that combines the nutty richness of pistachios with the natural sweetness of dates. These truffles are a no-bake dessert that's full of flavor and texture, with a soft, chewy center and a light crunch from the pistachios. The addition of almond butter helps bind the mixture together while adding an extra layer of richness. These truffles are packed with healthy fats, fiber, and protein, making them a great option for a quick energy boost or a satisfying after-dinner treat. With just a few simple ingredients, these truffles are easy to prepare and perfect for when you need a healthy, yet indulgent, snack.

Step by Step Preparation:

In a food processor, combine the pistachios, dates, shredded coconut, almond butter, vanilla extract, and sea salt. Process the mixture until it forms a sticky dough-like consistency. If the mixture feels too dry, add a little water, one teaspoon at a time, until it holds together. Once the mixture is ready, roll it into small balls, about 1 inch in diameter. Place the truffles on a parchment-lined tray and refrigerate them for at least 30 minutes to firm up. Once chilled, they are ready to enjoy. These truffles can be stored in an airtight container in the refrigerator for up to a week.

Chapter 6

Drinks

 ## INTRODUCTION TO REFRESHING DRINKS

There is something truly invigorating about a refreshing drink that satisfies the senses on a warm day or offers a revitalizing boost during the afternoon. We all know the feeling of reaching for something cool and refreshing, whether it is a chilled glass of iced tea, a fruit-infused water, or a smoothie that blends the best fruits and vegetables into a delicious and creamy beverage. Refreshing drinks are more than just a means of hydration. They offer a moment of enjoyment, a break from the busy rhythms of daily life, and a way to indulge in something both nourishing and delightful. A drink can be the highlight of your day, whether it is a freshly squeezed juice, an herbal iced tea, or a smoothie bowl full of vibrant colors and packed with nutrients. The beauty of refreshing drinks is their versatility. They can be sweet, tangy, or even savory, and they are the perfect way to hydrate while balancing your intake of essential vitamins, minerals, and hydration.

These drinks also provide an opportunity to explore different flavor profiles, textures, and combinations that can uplift your mood and support your body's needs. Whether it is the zing of citrus, the creamy smoothness of coconut milk, or the refreshing notes of mint, there are endless ingredients that can elevate a simple drink. There is something uniquely satisfying about creating a refreshing drink from scratch. You have complete control over what goes into it, ensuring it is made with real, wholesome ingredients without refined sugars or artificial additives. From detoxifying waters that flush out toxins to hydrating smoothies packed with antioxidants to energizing herbal teas that bring calm and focus, these drinks can meet your needs in a way that is both nourishing and enjoyable. You can hydrate, rejuvenate, and nourish your body while delighting your senses with every sip.

What makes these drinks so wonderful is their flexibility. They can be as simple or as complex as you want. A basic fruit-infused water with cucumber, lemon, and mint can be just as satisfying as a well-crafted smoothie blending superfoods like acai, chia seeds, or spirulina. There are no limits to the ways you can customize your own signature drink. You can mix various fruits and vegetables to create nutrient-packed smoothies that give you energy throughout the day or opt for something soothing like a cucumber and mint iced tea to cool off. Of course, the classic options are always a winner, such as a freshly squeezed glass of orange juice in the morning or coconut water with a hint of lime to keep you refreshed. The key is finding the right balance of flavors that not only taste amazing but also hydrate and nourish your body.

These drinks are a perfect example of how food and beverages can work together to benefit your overall health. Unlike sugary sodas or processed juices that are loaded with added sugars and preservatives, refreshing drinks made from whole fruits, herbs, and natural sweeteners provide your body with the nutrients it needs without any unnecessary additives. They help keep your body hydrated, support digestion, strengthen your immune system, and promote healthy skin. When you create your own drinks, you are taking a conscious step toward living a healthier lifestyle. Whether you are blending leafy greens, infusing water with fruits and herbs, or brewing a comforting cup of detox tea, refreshing drinks are an easy, delicious way to nourish your body from the inside out.

When it comes to staying hydrated, most people think of just water, but refreshing drinks offer so much more than plain water. Infused waters, for example, are an easy and flavorful way to boost hydration. By adding fruits, herbs, or even vegetables, you can transform your water into a delightful, nutrient-packed drink that keeps you feeling refreshed all day long. A simple combination of cucumber, lemon, and mint can make water feel like a spa experience in a glass. These drinks offer natural flavors that are satisfying without being overwhelming, and they can easily be customized to suit your tastes. You can create your own blends with ingredients that work best for your body, adding a burst of citrus, a touch of sweetness from berries, or a zing of ginger to help stimulate digestion. The possibilities are endless, making infused waters an ideal option for staying hydrated while enjoying a variety of flavors.

Smoothies are another popular choice when it comes to refreshing drinks, and they offer the benefit of being both hydrating and nutrient-rich. Smoothies allow you to blend fruits, vegetables, and other nutritious ingredients like seeds, nuts, or protein powders into a creamy, satisfying drink that's perfect for breakfast, lunch, or even a snack. The beauty of smoothies lies in their versatility, as they can be easily adapted to suit dietary preferences or restrictions. You can use dairy-free milk, add superfoods like spirulina or matcha, or even sneak in a handful of greens to make them a nourishing, antioxidant-packed meal. A fruit-based smoothie with banana, mango, and spinach can provide you with essential vitamins and minerals, while also satisfying your sweet tooth. For those looking to boost energy or support recovery, smoothies with added protein, healthy fats, or nut butter can help keep you feeling full and energized throughout the day.

Then there are the energizing herbal teas that offer a calming yet refreshing experience. These drinks not only provide hydration but also promote overall well-being. Herbal teas such as peppermint, chamomile, or ginger can aid digestion, soothe the stomach, and calm the mind, making them the perfect drink for winding down at the end of the day. Iced herbal teas are particularly refreshing when served cold, offering a revitalizing alternative to sugary sodas or store-bought juices. A cold brew of hibiscus or green tea can be a cooling, energizing drink that's packed with antioxidants, perfect for those seeking a healthier way to get a pick-me-up. You can experiment with different blends to discover your favorite flavors, and for an extra touch of sweetness, a drizzle of honey or a splash of lemon can enhance the natural flavors of your tea without overpowering them.

The key to creating the perfect refreshing drink is using whole, real ingredients that support your health. You don't need to rely on sugary, artificial additives to create a drink that satisfies your cravings and nourishes your body. By incorporating natural sweeteners like honey, stevia, or dates, you can enjoy the sweetness you love without the empty calories or blood sugar spikes associated with refined sugars. Adding ingredients like chia seeds, flaxseeds, and hemp hearts can provide extra fiber and omega-3 fatty acids, while antioxidant-rich berries or green vegetables give your drink a nutrient boost. The goal is to find a balance of flavors that taste good and also support your body's needs, whether that means boosting hydration, improving digestion, or providing sustained energy.

Incorporating these refreshing drinks into your daily routine is a simple yet effective way to stay hydrated and nourish your body with the nutrients it needs to thrive. They are a fun and easy way to experiment with flavors, textures, and ingredients, and they offer a variety of health benefits without the need for complicated preparation or expensive ingredients. Whether you are looking to detox, energize, or simply refresh, these drinks are a great way to enjoy something delicious while taking care of your body. So the next time you feel thirsty, skip the sugary beverages and try one of these flavorful, refreshing alternatives. Your body will thank you for it.

76. MORNING DETOX WATER

Servings:
2

Prep Time:
5 minutes

Chill Time:
1 hour

Ingredients:

- 1 cucumber (sliced)
- 1 lemon (sliced)
- 1 tablespoon grated ginger
- 5-6 fresh mint leaves
- 4 cups water, ice cubes (optional).

About the Dish:

Morning Detox Water is a refreshing and revitalizing drink designed to help kick-start your day while promoting hydration and digestion. The combination of cucumber, lemon, and ginger offers a refreshing burst of flavor that also aids in detoxification. Cucumber is known for its hydrating properties, lemon provides a boost of vitamin C, and ginger helps to stimulate digestion and reduce bloating. This drink can also help cleanse your system by flushing out toxins, making it the perfect beverage to start your morning and set the tone for a healthy day ahead.

Step by Step Preparation:

In a large pitcher, combine the cucumber, lemon slices, grated ginger, and mint leaves. Add the water and stir to combine. Let the mixture chill in the refrigerator for at least 1 hour to allow the flavors to infuse. Once chilled, pour over ice if desired, and enjoy this refreshing and detoxifying water. You can refill the pitcher with water throughout the day for continuous hydration.

77. CUCUMBER MINT SMOOTHIE

Servings:
2

Prep Time:
5 minutes

Ingredients:

- 1 cucumber (peeled and chopped)
- 1/2 cup fresh mint leaves
- 1/2 cup coconut water
- 1 tablespoon honey or maple syrup
- 1/2 cup Greek yogurt or plant-based yogurt, ice cubes.

About the Dish:

Cucumber Mint Smoothie is a cool, hydrating drink that blends the refreshing flavors of cucumber and mint with the creamy texture of yogurt. This smoothie is perfect for hot days or after a workout to cool down and rehydrate. The cucumber helps keep you hydrated, while the mint adds a refreshing touch and aids digestion. The coconut water brings in electrolytes, making this smoothie a great natural option for replenishment. The touch of honey or maple syrup balances the flavors without overpowering the natural freshness of the ingredients.

Step by Step Preparation:

Place the cucumber, fresh mint leaves, coconut water, honey (or maple syrup), and Greek yogurt in a blender. Add a few ice cubes and blend until smooth and creamy. Pour into glasses and garnish with a sprig of fresh mint. Serve immediately for a refreshing, hydrating treat.

78. GOLDEN MILK LATTE

Servings:	Prep Time:	Cook Time:
2	5 minutes	5 minutes

Ingredients:

- 2 cups unsweetened almond milk (or any plant-based milk)
- 1 teaspoon turmeric powder
- 1/2 teaspoon cinnamon
- 1 tablespoon honey or maple syrup
- 1/2 teaspoon ground ginger
- 1/4 teaspoon black pepper
- 1/2 teaspoon vanilla extract.

About the Dish:

Golden Milk Latte is a warming and soothing beverage made with turmeric, cinnamon, and ginger. This drink has anti-inflammatory properties and is packed with antioxidants. The addition of black pepper helps the body absorb the curcumin in turmeric, making this drink even more beneficial. Golden milk is not only comforting but also offers a natural boost to your immune system, making it the perfect evening drink to wind down or enjoy on a chilly day. The sweetness of honey or maple syrup adds balance to the earthy flavor of the spices.

Step by Step Preparation:

In a small saucepan, heat the almond milk over medium heat until warm but not boiling. Whisk in the turmeric, cinnamon, ginger, and black pepper. Stir in the honey or maple syrup and vanilla extract, then continue to whisk until the mixture is smooth and heated through. Pour into mugs and serve im-

mediately. Enjoy this soothing, anti-inflammatory drink as a nourishing treat any time of day.

79. GREEN TEA METABOLISM BOOSTER

Servings:	Prep Time:	Cook Time:
2	5 minutes	3 minutes

Ingredients:

- 2 cups green tea (brewed and cooled)
- 1/2 teaspoon matcha powder
- 1 tablespoon honey or stevia (optional)
- 1/2 lemon (juiced), a pinch of cayenne pepper.

About the Dish:

Green Tea Metabolism Booster is a simple yet powerful drink that blends the natural benefits of green tea with the metabolism-boosting properties of matcha and cayenne pepper. Green tea is known for its antioxidant properties and its ability to aid in fat burning, while matcha provides an additional boost of energy and concentration. The addition of lemon helps detoxify the body and enhances the flavors, while the cayenne pepper adds a spicy kick that stimulates circulation and further supports metabolism. This drink is perfect for those looking to kick-start their metabolism in the morning or as a midday energy booster.

Step by Step Preparation:

Brew the green tea and allow it to cool slightly. In a glass, whisk together the matcha powder and a little warm water to form a smooth paste. Add the brewed green tea to the matcha paste and stir until well combined. Squeeze in the lemon juice, and sweeten with honey or stevia if desired. Finish by adding a pinch of cayenne pepper and stir. Serve over ice for a refreshing and metabolism-boosting drink.

80. POMEGRANATE SPRITZER

Servings:	Prep Time:
4	5 minutes

Ingredients:

- 1 cup pomegranate juice (100% pure)
- 2 cups sparkling water
- 1 tablespoon lime juice
- 1-2 tablespoons honey or agave syrup (optional)
- fresh pomegranate seeds (for garnish)
- lime slices (for garnish).

About the Dish:

Pomegranate Spritzer is a fizzy and refreshing drink that brings together the tartness of pomegranate juice with the crispness of sparkling water. Pomegranate is packed with antioxidants and offers a naturally sweet yet tangy flavor. This spritzer is the perfect balance between sweet and tart, making it a refreshing and healthy option for any occasion. The lime juice adds a zesty twist, while the sparkling water creates a light and effervescent base. It's a perfect drink for hot summer days or as a fun and festive beverage for parties and gatherings.

Step by Step Preparation:

In a large pitcher, combine the pomegranate juice, sparkling water, and lime juice. Stir to combine, and add honey or agave syrup to taste if you pre-

fer a sweeter drink. Pour the spritzer into glasses filled with ice, and garnish with fresh pomegranate seeds and lime slices. Serve immediately and enjoy the refreshing, antioxidant-rich drink.

81. HOMEMADE GINGER LEMONADE

Servings:	Prep Time:	Cook Time:
4	10 minutes	5 minutes

Ingredients:

- 1-inch piece fresh ginger (peeled and sliced)
- 2 lemons (juiced)
- 4 cups water
- 2 tablespoons honey or maple syrup (adjust to taste), ice cubes.

About the Dish:

Homemade Ginger Lemonade is a perfect balance of refreshing and spicy. The natural heat from the ginger paired with the tartness of lemon creates a flavorful and invigorating drink that can help soothe an upset stomach, aid digestion, and provide a burst of hydration. Ginger is also known for its anti-inflammatory properties, while lemon offers vitamin C to help boost the immune system. This lemonade is a great alternative to sugary store-bought lemonades and is a healthier choice for quenching your thirst on warm days or when you need a little digestive support.

Step by Step Preparation:

In a small saucepan, bring 2 cups of water to a boil. Add the sliced ginger and simmer for 5 minutes, allowing the water to infuse with the ginger. Strain the liquid into a large pitcher, discarding the ginger slices. Add the lemon juice and honey or maple syrup to the pitcher, and stir until the sweetener is dissolved. Pour the remaining 2 cups of cold water into the pitcher and stir. Serve the ginger lemonade over ice, and enjoy this soothing and refreshing drink.

82. BEET AND BERRY JUICE

Servings:
2

Prep Time:
10 minutes

Ingredients:

- 1 small beetroot (peeled and chopped)
- 1/2 cup strawberries (fresh or frozen)
- 1/2 cup blueberries (fresh or frozen)
- 1/2 apple (cored and chopped)
- 1 tablespoon lemon juice
- 1 cup water or coconut water, ice cubes.

About the Dish:

Beet and Berry Juice is a vibrant and nutrient-packed drink that combines the earthy sweetness of beetroot with the fresh, antioxidant-rich flavors of berries. The beetroot helps to cleanse the liver and boost blood circulation, while the berries add a burst of vitamins, antioxidants, and natural sweetness. The apple and lemon juice brighten the flavors, making this juice both refreshing and revitalizing. It is a perfect choice for anyone looking to increase their daily intake of vegetables and fruits in a delicious and easy way.

Step by Step Preparation:

Place the chopped beetroot, strawberries, blueberries, and apple into a blender or juicer. Add the lemon juice and water or coconut water, and blend or juice until smooth. If you prefer a colder drink, add ice cubes to the blender before mixing. Pour the juice into glasses and serve immediately for a refreshing, nutrient-packed boost.

83. CARROT GINGER SMOOTHIE

Servings:
2

Prep Time:
5 minutes

Ingredients:

- 2 medium carrots (peeled and chopped)
- 1/2 inch piece fresh ginger (peeled)
- 1 banana (peeled)
- 1/2 cup orange juice (fresh or store-bought)
- 1/2 cup coconut milk (or any plant-based milk)
- 1 tablespoon honey or maple syrup (optional), ice cubes.

About the Dish:

Carrot Ginger Smoothie is a creamy and vibrant drink that combines the natural sweetness of carrots with the refreshing zing of ginger. The carrot provides beta-carotene, while the ginger adds a gentle spice and supports digestion. The banana creates a smooth texture, and the coconut milk adds creaminess without overpowering the flavors. This smoothie is a fantastic way to get your daily dose of vegetables while enjoying a deliciously satisfying drink. It's a perfect option for breakfast or a post-workout refuel.

Step by Step Preparation:

Place the carrots, ginger, banana, orange juice, and coconut milk into a blender. Add honey or maple syrup if you want to enhance the sweetness. Blend until smooth, adding ice cubes to achieve a colder and thicker consistency. Pour into glasses and enjoy this flavorful, nutrient-packed smoothie.

84. TURMERIC TONIC

Servings:	Prep Time:	Cook Time:
2	5 minutes	5 minutes

Ingredients:

- 1 cup water
- 1/2 teaspoon turmeric powder
- 1/2 teaspoon ground ginger
- 1 tablespoon honey or maple syrup
- 1/2 lemon (juiced)
- a pinch of black pepper (to enhance the absorption of turmeric).

About the Dish:

Turmeric Tonic is a potent and healing drink that combines the anti-inflammatory properties of turmeric with the soothing effects of ginger and lemon. This tonic is a perfect remedy for those looking to fight inflammation, improve digestion, and boost their immune system. The black pepper added to the tonic helps your body absorb turmeric's active ingredient, curcumin, making this tonic even more effective. The refreshing zing from the lemon and the natural sweetness from honey or maple syrup balance out the earthy flavors, creating a drink that is as enjoyable as it is beneficial.

Step by Step Preparation:

In a small saucepan, bring the water to a boil. Once boiling, remove from heat and whisk in the turmeric, ginger, and black pepper until well combined. Stir in the honey or maple syrup and lemon juice. Let the tonic cool slightly before serving. Drink it warm or at room temperature for a soothing, anti-inflammatory boost.

85. KOMBUCHA BREW

Servings:	Prep Time:	Fermentation Time:
4	10 minutes	7-10 days

Ingredients:

- 1 SCOBY (Symbiotic Culture of Bacteria and Yeast)
- 1/2 cup sugar
- 4 bags black tea
- 4 cups water
- 1/4 cup starter tea (from a previous batch of kombucha or store-bought).

About the Dish:

Kombucha Brew is a fermented tea drink that's known for its tangy flavor and numerous health benefits. The process of fermentation allows beneficial probiotics to develop, which can help with digestion and improve gut health. Kombucha is also packed with antioxidants and can provide a natural energy boost without the caffeine jitters associated with coffee. This drink is a great alternative to sugary sodas, offering a refreshing and healthy option with a unique flavor profile. The beauty of kombucha is that you can flavor it however you like once it's brewed and fermented, adding fruits, herbs, or spices to customize your own batch.

Step by Step Preparation:

Start by boiling the water and dissolving the sugar into it. Once the sugar has dissolved, add the tea bags and steep the tea for about 10 minutes. Allow the tea to cool to room temperature. Once cooled, pour the tea into a clean glass jar and add the starter tea. Gently add the SCOBY to the jar, ensuring it floats on the surface. Cover the jar with a clean cloth and secure it with a rubber band. Let the kombucha ferment for 7-10 days in a warm, dark place. After the fermentation period, taste the kombucha. If it has reached your desired tanginess, remove the SCOBY and save it for the next batch. You can then bottle the kombucha and refrigerate it. Optional: Add fruit or herbs to flavor the kombucha before bottling. Enjoy your homemade kombucha as a refreshing and healthy beverage!

Chapter 7

The 21-Day Meal Plan

 ## WEEK 1: KICKSTARTING WELLNESS

Starting a wellness journey is a personal decision, one that often feels both exciting and overwhelming at the same time. The first week of any lifestyle change is essential because it sets the tone for everything that follows. It is during this week that we begin to establish new habits that will support our health and well-being in the long term. Instead of focusing on perfection, the goal of Week 1 is to lay a strong foundation for your wellness journey, with an emphasis on small, manageable steps that can bring about meaningful changes. These early days are about nurturing your body, reintroducing balance, and making choices that will gradually lead you to the healthier lifestyle you desire. You do not need to rush. Every step you take toward a healthier lifestyle is a victory.

One of the most powerful tools you can embrace in Week 1 is hydration. Many of us do not drink enough water on a daily basis, and that can have a significant impact on our energy, digestion, and overall health. Proper hydration helps to flush toxins from the body, boosts cognitive function, and supports skin health. This week, aim to increase your water intake. Start each morning by drinking a glass of water to rehydrate your body after hours of sleep. Carry a reusable water bottle throughout the day to make it easier to stay on track with your hydration goals. If you find plain water unappealing, try adding fresh ingredients like cucumber, lemon, or mint for a burst of flavor. Additionally, herbal teas or infused waters can be a great way to support hydration while offering a variety of health benefits. These drinks can help calm the body, provide antioxidants, and support digestion.

Nutrition is another area to focus on in Week 1, as it plays a crucial role in how we feel physically and mentally. A diet rich in whole, unprocessed foods can provide your body with the necessary nutrients it needs to function optimally. Begin by incorporating more fruits, vegetables, whole grains, and lean proteins into your meals. Aim to eat a variety of colorful vegetables and fruits, as they provide a wide range of vitamins, minerals, and antioxidants that help to combat inflammation, boost immunity, and improve overall health. Whole grains like quinoa, brown rice, and oats offer fiber and energy, while lean proteins from sources like chicken, fish, beans, and tofu help build muscle and repair tissues. By focusing on nutrient-dense foods, you are giving your body the fuel it needs to thrive.

Meal prepping is an excellent way to stay consistent with your nutrition goals. Planning and preparing meals ahead of time can make all the difference in ensuring that you have healthy, balanced options readily available. It helps to eliminate the temptation to reach for processed or unhealthy alternatives when you are hungry or in a rush. Try setting aside time each week to chop vegetables, cook grains, or prepare simple dishes that you can easily heat up when needed. This will save you time and energy during the week while keeping you on track with your healthy eating goals. It also allows you to experiment with new recipes and discover meals you enjoy, which will help you stay motivated and excited about your wellness journey.

In addition to focusing on hydration and nutrition, Week 1 is the perfect time to begin establishing healthy sleep habits. Sleep is essential for recovery, energy, and mental clarity. Without enough restful sleep, your body struggles to function at its best. Quality sleep supports immune function, aids in weight management, and improves emotional health. Start by establishing a bedtime routine that helps signal to your body that it is time to wind down. This can include activities such as reading, stretching, or meditating. Avoid screens like your phone, tablet, or computer at least 30 minutes before bed, as they can interfere with your body's production of melatonin, the hormone that regulates sleep. Create a calming environment in your bedroom by keeping it cool, dark, and quiet. The more consistent you are with your sleep routine, the better your body will adjust and begin to reap the benefits of quality rest.

Physical activity is also a key component of your wellness journey. This first week does not require intense workouts, but it's important to start moving your body in ways that feel good and are sustainable. Focus on light activities such as walking, yoga, or stretching. These activities not only help improve flexibility and muscle tone but also reduce stress, promote better sleep, and boost mood. Aim to get at least 30 minutes of movement most days of the week. You don't need to push yourself too hard; simply getting moving each day will have long-lasting benefits. You may also want to try simple at-home workouts like bodyweight exercises, which are easy to do and require no equipment. Remember, the key to lasting wellness is consistency. Small daily actions add up over time and help create habits that are manageable and sustainable.

Mental well-being is just as important as physical health, and it's something to nurture throughout Week 1. Start by practicing mindfulness to bring your awareness to the present moment and to help you better manage stress. This could be through deep breathing exercises, guided meditations, or simply taking time during the day to focus on the sensations around you. Journaling is another great tool for mental clarity. By writing down your thoughts, reflections, and goals, you can process your emotions and create a positive, mindful approach to your day. Taking time for yourself each day, even if it's just a few minutes, can help clear mental clutter and keep you focused on your wellness journey.

Social connections also play a significant role in your overall wellness. Week 1 is a great time to evaluate the relationships in your life and find ways to foster those that are positive and supportive. Whether it's spending quality time with family, connecting with friends, or joining a wellness community, making an effort to build relationships that nourish your spirit will improve your emotional well-being. Sharing your wellness goals with others can also be a source of encouragement and accountability. When you feel supported, you're more likely to stay committed to your journey and enjoy the process.

As you complete Week 1, remember to celebrate your progress. Whether it's drinking more water, preparing healthier meals, or getting better sleep, each step you take is a victory. The foundation you are building this week will lead to lasting changes. You are not expected to be perfect, and there is no rush. The focus should be on making small, sustainable changes that become part of your everyday life. Week 1 is just the beginning, but it's a crucial first step toward building a healthier, more balanced lifestyle. Every positive change, no matter how small, will lead you closer to your wellness goals.

WEEK 2: DEEPENING THE JOURNEY

After completing the first week of your wellness journey, you may have already started to feel the benefits of the changes you've made. Week 2 is about deepening those efforts and building on the foundation you've laid. The goal is to take what you've learned and integrate it further into your daily routine, solidifying these habits as a natural part of your lifestyle. This week is an opportunity to refine your practices and push yourself a bit further, but always with the understanding that progress, not perfection, is the goal. It is about continuing to honor your body and your needs while exploring deeper connections to your health and wellness.

One of the first areas to revisit in Week 2 is hydration. By now, you've likely established a habit of drinking more water. This week, focus on varying the ways in which you hydrate to keep things exciting and to ensure you are still meeting your hydration goals. Try infusing your water with different fruits and herbs. Some options include citrus fruits like lemon, lime, and orange, or herbs like basil, rosemary, or mint. These additions not only add flavor but also offer additional health benefits. Citrus fruits are full of vitamin C, which supports your immune system, while herbs can provide antioxidants and anti-inflammatory properties. You can also experiment with coconut water or herbal teas like chamomile or peppermint for a change of pace. A refreshing drink like cucumber-infused water can also be great for digestion and promoting a feeling of fullness.

This week is a great time to expand your nutrition by focusing on more plant-based meals. Incorporating more plant-based foods, such as beans, lentils, whole grains, and leafy greens, will provide your body with the nutrients it needs without the added fat or cholesterol that can come from animal-based products. Plant-based foods are rich in fiber, vitamins, and minerals, which are essential for keeping your digestive system running smoothly and your energy levels high. Experiment with new recipes that incorporate these foods, like a hearty vegetable stir-fry, a nutrient-packed salad with quinoa, or a comforting lentil soup. By adding more plant-based meals to your week, you can improve your digestion, reduce inflammation, and feel more energized throughout the day.

As you refine your nutrition, Week 2 is also a great time to begin practicing mindful eating. This practice involves slowing down and paying attention to the food you are eating—how it tastes, how it makes you feel, and how much of it you actually need. Many people eat on autopilot, distracted by TV, phones, or other things, but mindful eating encourages you to focus on the present moment and enjoy the experience of eating. It allows you to tune in to your body's hunger and fullness cues, which can help you make better choices and prevent overeating. To practice mindful eating, try sitting down at a table for each meal, free of distractions. Take the time to chew your food thoroughly and savor the flavors. This simple practice can help you develop a healthier relationship with food and deepen your connection to your body's needs.

Along with mindful eating, this week also offers an opportunity to pay closer attention to your exercise routine. Now that you have had a week to adjust, you can gradually increase the intensity or duration of your workouts. If you have been walking or doing light stretching, try adding a few short bursts of cardio or increasing the duration of your sessions. If you have already been doing more intense exercise, challenge yourself to explore new activities, such as swimming, cycling, or strength training. You might also want to add more variety to your workouts by trying something new, such as a dance class, yoga, or even a hike in nature. By changing up your exercise routine, you can prevent burnout and keep things fresh and exciting while continuing to build strength, endurance, and flexibility.

In Week 2, it is important to not only focus on your physical health but also to nurture your mental and emotional well-being. At this point, you may be feeling more energized and motivated, but it is just as important to take time for self-care and reflection. Mental health plays a vital role in overall wellness, and taking the time to relax, unwind, and reflect can help keep you grounded. You can deepen your mindfulness practice, try guided meditation, or simply take time to breathe and center yourself throughout the day. Journaling is also a great way to track your emotions, goals, and progress, allowing you to reflect on how far you have come and what you want to achieve moving forward. By focusing on mental wellness alongside physical health, you create a more balanced and holistic approach to your wellness journey.

Another key focus in Week 2 is improving sleep quality. As you continue to prioritize your health, sleep plays a critical role in recovery and maintaining energy levels. If you have not yet established a consistent sleep routine, this week is the time to do so. Set a regular bedtime and wake-up time to regulate your body's internal clock. Ensure your sleep environment is as restful as possible by minimizing distractions. Try using blackout curtains to block out light and avoid using electronic devices before bed. If you struggle with falling asleep, consider adding calming practices like reading, meditation, or a warm bath to your evening routine. Consistent, restorative sleep will help you recharge and feel your best throughout the week.

By the time Week 3 arrives in your wellness journey, you may have begun to notice the positive changes in your physical and mental state. The first two weeks were all about laying the foundation, and now it's time to build on that foundation and deepen your commitment to lasting change. Week 3 is an opportunity to embrace the changes you've made, solidify them as part of your routine, and take the next step toward becoming the healthiest version of yourself. It is a time to reflect on how far you have come and to push forward with the confidence that the new habits you have cultivated will continue to support your wellness goals.

A crucial element of Week 3 is mindset. When you start a wellness journey, you begin with the idea that something needs to change, and you set out to make those changes. Now, in Week 3, it is time to fully embrace your mindset and approach to health. At this stage, your body has adjusted to the changes you've made, and your routine has likely started to feel more natural. Now it's time to focus on strengthening the mental aspect of your wellness journey. A positive mindset is a critical component of long-term success. Week 3 offers you the chance to explore how your thoughts shape your actions. Remind yourself of your purpose, your "why," and reconnect with the goals you set in the beginning. Whether your goal is to have more energy, improve your physical health, or feel more balanced in your daily life, reflecting on your reasons will reignite your motivation and keep you going.

The power of mindset extends beyond just your physical changes. It also affects how you deal with obstacles along the way. Understand that perfection is not the goal. Life is full of challenges and setbacks, and some days will be harder than others. Week 3 is about learning to accept that you don't have to be perfect to make progress. When things don't go as planned, rather than feeling discouraged, take a moment to pause and acknowledge your progress. Every step you take is part of the journey, and each day that you continue to show up for yourself is a success. When you encounter setbacks, use them as learning experiences, not as reasons to give up. Acknowledge any difficulties with self-compassion and move forward, knowing that you are still on track to achieving your goals. This shift in mindset will help you stay focused and resilient throughout the journey.

As you embrace these changes, it's important to focus on your nutrition. Week 3 is a good time to assess your diet and see how you can continue to improve your eating habits. By now, you may have begun to settle into a routine that includes more whole foods, fruits, vegetables, and lean proteins. This week, challenge yourself to take your nutrition to the next level by adding more variety to your meals. Experiment with new fruits, vegetables, or even spices to bring excitement to your plate. Different colors on your plate mean different nutrients, so aim to include a wide range of fruits and vegetables that are rich in fiber, vitamins, and minerals.

Consider incorporating more plant-based meals into your diet. Eating a more plant-based diet is not only good for your health but also beneficial for the environment. Start by incorporating more beans, lentils, and plant-based proteins into your meals. There are many delicious, hearty plant-based dishes that will nourish your body while offering a satisfying meal. Try making a lentil stew, a vegetable stir-fry, or a nourishing quinoa salad. Including these meals will provide your body with the fiber and nutrients needed to improve digestion, boost energy levels, and reduce inflammation. It is important to remember that every meal doesn't need to be plant-based, but adding these foods into your weekly rotation can have a significant impact on your health.

Along with nutrition, Week 3 is a perfect time to focus on practicing mindful eating. This means slowing down and paying attention to how your food makes you feel. Mindful eating helps you become more in tune with your body's hunger and fullness cues. By eating slowly and without distractions, you can better understand when you are truly hungry and when you are satisfied. Avoid eating while watching TV or scrolling through your phone, as this can lead to overeating without even realizing it. Practice eating your meals in a quiet, peaceful environment. Sit down, chew your food thoroughly, and savor each bite. By making this shift, you can strengthen your relationship with food, reduce mindless eating, and improve digestion.

As you continue to improve your nutrition, Week 3 is also a great time to increase the intensity of your workouts. By now, you've had time to establish a routine and assess what types of exercise you enjoy. Now, it's time to gradually challenge your body with more intense or varied physical activities. If you've been walking, yoga, or stretching, try incorporating more vigorous exercise such as jogging, cycling, or strength training. Adding variety to your workouts will keep things exciting and help you target different muscle groups. If you've been focusing on one type of exercise, this is the time to try something new, such as swimming, Pilates, or dance classes. Introducing new activities will help prevent boredom and keep your body progressing toward your fitness goals. Aim to incorporate both strength and cardio exercises into your routine to improve your endurance and overall strength.

Physical activity doesn't always have to be intense. If you feel like you need to scale back, make sure to include rest days in your week. Rest is a vital component of any fitness routine. It allows your muscles to recover and grow stronger, while also preventing burnout. Week 3 should focus on finding a balance between pushing yourself and allowing time for recovery. Listen to your body and give yourself permission to rest when needed. As you become more attuned to your body's signals, you will find it easier to determine when to push yourself and when to take it easy.

In addition to your physical and nutritional health, it's important to continue nurturing your mental well-being. Week 3 offers you the opportunity to enhance your mental health by practicing stress management techniques and fostering positive thinking. This week, try incorporating more mindfulness exercises such as deep breathing, meditation, or journaling into your routine. These activities can help reduce stress, improve focus, and enhance your overall well-being. Make time each day for self-care, whether it's taking a few moments to journal, going for a walk in nature, or simply breathing deeply to clear your mind. Regularly practicing mindfulness will help you stay present and maintain mental clarity, which is essential for navigating the challenges that come with making lasting life changes.

As you embrace these changes and deepen your commitment to your wellness journey, remember that growth takes time. Be kind to yourself as you navigate Week 3, and celebrate the progress you've made. By staying consistent and embracing your new lifestyle, you are building habits that will last a lifetime. Each day is a step closer to achieving your wellness goals, and with each positive change, you are creating a stronger foundation for long-term health and happiness.

🍇 DAILY MEAL PLANNER

A well-structured daily meal planner plays an important role in supporting your wellness goals. It allows you to plan your meals ahead of time, ensuring that you consistently make healthier choices throughout the day. By planning your meals, you can save time and reduce the stress of deciding what to eat last minute. It helps prevent unhealthy, last-minute decisions and encourages the inclusion of nutrient-dense foods. Having a plan also provides an opportunity to make sure that your meals contain the proper balance of protein, carbohydrates, fats, and fiber to keep you feeling satisfied and energized all day long.

Breakfast is the first opportunity of the day to nourish your body. It should include a combination of protein, healthy fats, and fiber to keep you full and energized. A well-balanced breakfast might include a smoothie packed with fruits, vegetables, and protein powder, or perhaps a bowl of oatmeal topped with nuts and seeds. These options provide lasting energy without the sugar spikes and crashes often associated with processed breakfast foods.

Lunch is a key meal for sustaining your energy levels through the afternoon. A balanced lunch should include lean protein sources like grilled chicken, tofu, or beans, along with fiber-rich vegetables and whole grains. It is a good idea to make lunches that are easily portable, so you can take them with you to work or school. A salad made with leafy greens, roasted vegetables, and quinoa, topped with olive oil and lemon juice, can be a refreshing and nutrient-packed choice. Adding a healthy fat, like avocado or nuts, can help make the meal more filling and satisfying.

Dinner is a time to enjoy a lighter meal that supports relaxation before bedtime. While it's important to have a balanced meal, dinner can be slightly lighter than lunch. It should still contain a good portion of lean protein, such as grilled fish or a plant-based option like lentils. Pair it with non-starchy vegetables like steamed broccoli, zucchini, or cauliflower, and a small portion of whole grains such as brown rice or quinoa. This combination helps ensure you are full, without overloading your body with heavy foods before sleep.

Snacking throughout the day can help bridge the gap between meals and provide an energy boost. Healthy snacks might include nuts and seeds, fruit with nut butter, or a handful of vegetables with hummus. These snacks should provide you with both protein and fiber, helping to keep you satisfied and avoid mid-day cravings for less healthy options. Staying prepared with healthy snacks can keep you on track and prevent you from reaching for sugary or processed foods when hunger strikes.

Having a daily meal planner allows you to be intentional about your food choices, making it easier to stay aligned with your health goals and avoid poor decisions. It also helps ensure that your body receives the proper nutrients to feel good, perform well, and maintain energy levels. By dedicating time to planning your meals, you can develop a consistent routine that will serve you well in the long term, creating a solid foundation for overall well-being.

🛒 SHOPPING LISTS

A well-organized shopping list is an essential tool for maintaining a healthy and balanced diet. It helps streamline your grocery shopping, ensures you only buy what you need, and keeps you focused on purchasing nutritious ingredients. With a shopping list, you are more likely to avoid impulse buys and can stay on track with your wellness goals. By planning ahead, you can ensure that you have everything you need for the week, which makes meal preparation more efficient and less stressful.

When creating a shopping list, it's important to consider the meals you plan to prepare for the week. Start by listing all the ingredients you need for breakfast, lunch, dinner, and snacks. This will help you identify items that you may already have in your pantry or fridge, allowing you to avoid unnecessary purchases. By planning meals ahead of time, you can buy in bulk for items like grains, beans, and vegetables, which are often versatile and can be used in a variety of meals throughout the week.

A key aspect of a healthy shopping list is focusing on whole, unprocessed foods. Fresh fruits and vegetables should be at the top of your list. Aim for a variety of colorful vegetables such as leafy greens, bell peppers, tomatoes, and cruciferous vegetables like broccoli or cauliflower. These provide essential vitamins, minerals, and antioxidants that support overall health. Include a range of fruits as well, such as berries, apples, oranges, and bananas, to ensure you're getting both variety and the nutrients your body needs.

Next, consider the proteins you will include in your meals. This might include lean meats like chicken, turkey, or fish, or plant-based proteins like beans, lentils, tofu, and tempeh. Adding a variety of protein sources to your shopping list ensures that you can create balanced meals that support muscle repair and keep you feeling full throughout the day.

Grains are also an important part of a healthy diet, providing fiber and energy. Whole grains such as quinoa, brown rice, oats, and whole wheat pasta should be staples in your shopping list. These grains are nutrient-dense and serve as the base for many meals, helping to fuel your body and keep you satisfied.

Healthy fats are another key component of a well-rounded diet. Include foods like olive oil, avocados, nuts, and seeds in your shopping list. These fats support heart health, brain function, and keep you feeling full and satisfied. Consider adding nut butter, coconut oil, or chia seeds as versatile options to enhance your meals or snacks.

Don't forget the dairy or dairy alternatives you may need. If you consume dairy, include options like yogurt, cheese, or milk. For those following plant-based diets, there are many dairy alternatives available, such as almond milk, coconut yogurt, or nutritional yeast. These can provide the same creamy texture and calcium benefits.

Finally, make sure to stock up on herbs, spices, and condiments to add flavor to your meals without relying on processed sauces or sugar. Fresh herbs like basil, cilantro, and parsley, along with dried spices like turmeric, cumin, and cinnamon, can turn a simple dish into a flavorful, nutrient-packed meal.

With a well-planned shopping list, you can make your grocery shopping more efficient, less stressful, and aligned with your health goals. It allows you to stick to your budget, avoid purchasing unhealthy options, and ensure you have everything you need to make nourishing meals for the week.

Chapter 8

Additional Resources

 ## TIPS FOR SUSTAINABLE EATING

Sustainable eating is about making choices that are not only good for your health but also better for the environment. It's about being mindful of how the foods we consume impact the planet and choosing foods that contribute to a healthier world for future generations. By adopting sustainable eating practices, we can reduce food waste, conserve natural resources, and minimize our carbon footprint. Here are some tips to help you eat sustainably while still enjoying delicious, nourishing meals.

1. Focus on Plant-Based Foods

One of the most effective ways to eat sustainably is by incorporating more plant-based foods into your diet. Plant-based foods like vegetables, fruits, legumes, and whole grains typically have a lower environmental impact than animal-based foods. Growing plants generally requires fewer resources such as water and land, and it produces fewer greenhouse gases. By eating more plant-based meals, you can significantly reduce your carbon footprint and contribute to the health of the planet. You don't have to eliminate animal products entirely, but reducing your intake can make a positive impact. Try experimenting with plant-based proteins like beans, lentils, tofu, and tempeh, which are delicious and full of nutrients.

2. Buy Local and Seasonal Produce

When you choose local and seasonal produce, you're not only supporting local farmers, but you are also reducing the environmental costs associated with shipping food over long distances. Produce that is grown locally tends to be fresher, more nutritious, and less reliant on harmful pesticides and chemicals. Seasonal foods often require fewer artificial interventions to grow, as they are in sync with the natural environment. To find out what's in season, consider visiting a local farmer's market or joining a community-supported agriculture (CSA) program. Eating seasonally also encourages variety in your diet, as you'll be eating foods that are naturally at their peak flavor and nutrition.

3. Reduce Food Waste

Reducing food waste is one of the simplest yet most impactful sustainable eating habits you can adopt. It's estimated that nearly one-third of the food produced in the world is wasted, which contributes to unnecessary environmental strain. You can minimize waste by planning your meals in advance, using up leftovers, and properly storing food to prolong its freshness. Consider using vegetable scraps, such as potato peels, carrot tops, or broccoli stems, to make broths, soups, or smoothies. Be creative with your cooking to ensure that food is used in its entirety, which will not only help the environment but also save you money.

4. Choose Sustainable Seafood

When incorporating seafood into your diet, it's important to choose sustainably sourced options. Overfishing is a major concern for the health of oceans and marine life. By selecting fish and shellfish that are certified by organizations like the Marine Stewardship Council (MSC), you're helping to support sustainable fishing practices that protect marine ecosystems. You can also consider plant-based alternatives like seaweed or algae, which are rich in nutrients and have a much lower environmental impact. If you do consume seafood, look for options that are harvested or farmed in environmentally responsible ways.

5. Minimize Packaging and Buy in Bulk

Packaging waste is a significant issue, particularly plastic packaging, which contributes to pollution and harms wildlife. To reduce packaging waste, consider buying in bulk whenever possible. Bulk bins at grocery stores often offer grains, legumes, nuts, and spices without unnecessary packaging, allowing you to reduce single-use plastic consumption. Bringing your own reusable bags, containers, and jars to the store also helps reduce waste. Whenever possible, choose products that are packaged in recyclable, biodegradable, or reusable materials. Supporting stores that prioritize sustainable packaging can also encourage larger businesses to adopt more environmentally friendly practices.

6. Grow Your Own Food

Growing your own food, even if it's just a small herb garden on your windowsill, is a rewarding and sustainable practice. Growing your own produce reduces the need for store-bought items, minimizes transportation-related carbon footprints, and allows you to control the methods used in cultivating your food. If you have the space, you can grow vegetables like tomatoes, lettuce, cucumbers, and peppers, which are easy to care for and provide fresh, organic ingredients. If you live in an apartment or have limited outdoor space, try starting with herbs like basil, mint, or parsley, which can be grown indoors in small pots. Gardening is a sustainable practice that fosters a deeper connection to where food comes from and encourages a more mindful approach to eating.

7. Choose Organic When Possible

Organic farming practices are typically gentler on the environment, as they avoid the use of synthetic pesticides and fertilizers that can harm soil health, water quality, and biodiversity. While organic products may be more expensive, making small shifts toward organic choices for foods you consume most often—such as leafy greens, berries, or dairy—can be a great start. By choosing organic, you're not only helping to protect the environment but also supporting agricultural practices that promote biodiversity and healthy ecosystems.

8. Drink More Water and Reduce Sugary Drinks

Drinking water instead of sugary drinks like soda or packaged fruit juices is a simple way to improve your health while reducing environmental waste. Sugary drinks contribute to unnecessary packaging waste, especially plastic bottles, and require a significant amount of resources to produce. Water, on the other hand, is free from waste and is the healthiest option for hydration. You can make your water more exciting by infusing it with fruits, herbs, or spices like cucumber, lemon, or mint. This helps you reduce reliance on bottled drinks while also supporting your body's hydration needs.

9. Support Ethical Food Brands

When shopping for packaged food items, choose brands that prioritize sustainability and ethical practices. Many food companies are making strides toward sourcing ingredients responsibly, using sustainable packaging, and ensuring fair working conditions for their employees. Look for certifications like Fair Trade, Rainforest Alliance, or B Corp when making food purchases. Supporting ethical brands encourages the larger food industry to adopt more sustainable practices, helping to create a more sustainable food system.

10. Mind Your Portions

Overeating is not only detrimental to your health but also contributes to food waste. Many people tend to over-serve or over-prepare food, which leads to uneaten meals that go to waste. To avoid this, practice mindful portion control by serving smaller amounts and being mindful of how much food you actually need. You can always go back for more if you're still hungry. This practice helps reduce food waste and ensures you're eating the right amount to maintain your health and well-being.

By embracing sustainable eating practices, you can contribute to a healthier planet and a healthier you. Simple shifts in how and what you eat can make a significant difference in the environmental impact of your diet. Every small step toward sustainable eating counts, and as more people adopt these practices, the collective impact can be profound. Start with a few tips and gradually incorporate them into your routine, and you'll be making a positive change for both yourself and the environment.

HOW TO SOURCE INGREDIENTS LOCALLY

Sourcing ingredients locally is not only an excellent way to support your community and the environment but also a way to enjoy fresher, more nutritious produce. By choosing locally grown foods, you can contribute to a more sustainable food system while enjoying seasonal, high-quality ingredients that support your health. Here are some practical ways to source ingredients locally and incorporate them into your daily meals.

1. Visit Farmers' Markets

One of the best ways to find local ingredients is to visit your local farmers' market. These markets offer a wide variety of fresh produce, meats, dairy products, and other local goods directly from farmers and artisans. At a farmers' market, you are more likely to find seasonal fruits and vegetables that are grown nearby, without the need for long-distance transportation. Many markets also sell honey, homemade preserves, fresh herbs, and other specialty items that you can't always find in regular grocery stores. Visiting the market not only allows you to support local growers, but it also gives you the opportunity to ask questions about how the food is grown and what methods are used, helping you make more informed choices about the food you buy.

2. Join a Community-Supported Agriculture (CSA) Program

Another great way to source local ingredients is by joining a Community-Supported Agriculture (CSA) program. A CSA allows you to purchase a share of a farm's harvest for a set period, typically during the growing season. Each week, you'll receive a box filled with freshly harvested produce, which may include a variety of seasonal fruits, vegetables, and even eggs or dairy. By subscribing to a CSA, you are directly supporting local farmers and receiving the freshest ingredients possible. This can be a convenient option for those who want to eat more locally but might not have the time to visit farmers' markets regularly. CSAs are often more affordable than buying organic produce from the store, and they can help you discover new foods and recipes to try throughout the season.

3. Shop at Local Grocery Stores with a Focus on Local Products

While many grocery stores focus on global supply chains, there are often local or regional sections within the store that highlight produce and products grown close to home. Look for grocery stores that prioritize sourcing from local farms and businesses. Many stores now feature a "locally grown" or "farm fresh" section where you can find seasonal vegetables, fruits, meats, dairy, and other products. These stores often work directly with local farmers and suppliers to stock their shelves with high-quality, fresh ingredients. Shopping at these stores can help reduce the environmental impact of transporting food over long distances while ensuring that the produce you buy is fresh and in season.

4. Grow Your Own Food

If you have the space and time, growing your own food is one of the most sustainable ways to source ingredients locally. Even if you don't have a large garden, you can grow herbs, small vegetables, and fruits in containers on a balcony or windowsill. Growing your own food not only gives you access to the freshest ingredients, but it also reduces the carbon footprint associated with buying food from the store. Start with easy-to-grow plants like tomatoes, lettuce, peppers, basil, and mint. You can also grow your own herbs in small pots and keep them in your kitchen or on a sunny windowsill. When you grow your own food, you have complete control over the growing process and can use sustainable methods to reduce your environmental impact.

5. Support Local Butchers, Fishmongers, and Artisanal Producers

Sourcing local ingredients goes beyond just fruits and vegetables. Many local butchers, fishmongers, and artisans offer high-quality meats, fish, eggs, and dairy products that are raised or produced nearby. Supporting these small businesses not only ensures that the products are fresh but also helps promote ethical and sustainable farming practices. Local meat and fish are often produced with fewer chemicals, hormones, and antibiotics than their mass-produced counterparts. Additionally, local artisans may produce cheeses, breads, or preserves using traditional methods that support local food culture and reduce the environmental impact of mass production.

6. Explore Pick-Your-Own Farms

Pick-your-own farms are an excellent way to source fresh, local ingredients, especially during peak harvest seasons. Many farms allow customers to come in and pick their own fruits and vegetables, such as strawberries, apples, pumpkins, or tomatoes. This provides a fun and educational experience while ensuring that you're getting the freshest, most seasonal produce possible. By picking the ingredients yourself, you also reduce packaging waste and avoid purchasing items that may have been transported over long distances. It's a wonderful way to connect with the land, support local farms, and teach children or family members about where food comes from.

7. Forage Locally

Foraging for wild foods is an option for those who are interested in finding locally grown ingredients in their natural habitats. Wild edibles, such as wild berries, mushrooms, and herbs, can often be found in forests, fields, and even urban areas. However, foraging requires knowledge and care, as some plants are poisonous or endangered. If you're new to foraging, it's a good idea to join a foraging group or take a class to learn about the safe and responsible collection of wild foods. Foraging can be a rewarding way to connect with nature while sourcing fresh and unique ingredients for your meals.

8. Connect with Local Food Co-Ops and Online Marketplaces

Local food cooperatives (co-ops) and online marketplaces dedicated to supporting local food sources are excellent alternatives to traditional grocery stores. Many co-ops allow members to purchase food in bulk directly from local farms or suppliers, often at discounted prices. Online marketplaces are also making it easier to source local products by allowing farmers to sell their goods directly to consumers. These platforms often have wide varieties of locally produced food items, from fresh produce to homemade products, and they can help you connect with food producers in your area.

9. Educate Yourself About Local Food Systems

To effectively source ingredients locally, it helps to understand your area's food systems. Research local farms, food hubs, and food programs that support sustainable agriculture and local producers. Websites, local food guides, or even social media groups dedicated to local food sources can be valuable resources in connecting with farmers and food suppliers near you. Being proactive in learning about your local food network will allow you to make better choices and foster stronger connections with the people who grow your food.

UNDERSTANDING FOOD LABELS

Food labels are an essential tool when it comes to making informed choices about the food we eat. With so many products available in grocery stores today, understanding food labels can help us navigate through the clutter and select the options that best align with our health goals. Food labels provide critical information about the nutritional content, ingredients, and sourcing of food products. They can help you determine the quality of a product, its calorie content, its levels of fat and sugar, and more. Being able to read and interpret these labels correctly empowers you to make better, healthier choices for yourself and your family.

Nutritional Information

The nutritional facts panel is one of the most important sections of a food label. This panel typically includes the number of servings per container, the serving size, and the nutritional breakdown per serving. It is important to pay attention to serving sizes because the nutritional information provided on the label is based on one serving, not the entire package. A common mistake is thinking that a whole container of a product equals one serving, which can lead to misjudging the actual number of calories, fats, and other nutrients consumed.

The panel will also list total calories, including the breakdown of calories from fat, along with the amounts of fat, carbohydrates, and protein per serving. There are different types of fats to watch out for, including saturated fats and trans fats. Saturated fats, found in foods like butter and fatty meats, should be consumed in moderation, while trans fats, often found in processed foods, should be avoided as much as possible. Aim for foods that are low in saturated fat and free of trans fats, as these can negatively impact heart health.

Carbohydrates are also an essential nutrient listed on food labels. They include sugars, fibers, and starches. It is important to distinguish between the different types of carbohydrates, especially the "added sugars." Natural sugars, like those found in fruits and vegetables, are generally considered healthy, while added sugars found in processed foods and drinks can lead to weight gain, obesity, and chronic diseases like diabetes. Look for foods that are low in added sugars and high in fiber, which supports digestion and helps maintain steady energy levels throughout the day.

The protein content listed on the label can also help you assess whether a food is providing adequate amounts of this essential nutrient. Protein is crucial for muscle repair, immune function, and overall growth, so it is important to include a sufficient amount in your diet.

Ingredient List

The ingredient list is another important part of the food label. It tells you exactly what is inside the product. Ingredients are listed in order of quantity, from the most abundant to the least abundant. If sugar or unhealthy fats are listed among the first few ingredients, it is usually a sign that the product is highly processed and not a great choice. Foods with simple, recognizable ingredients like whole grains, vegetables, fruits, and lean proteins are typically better options than foods with long ingredient lists full of chemicals, preservatives, and artificial additives.

If you are following a specific dietary regimen or have food allergies, the ingredient list can help you identify ingredients that you need to avoid. Many food labels now feature allergen information at the bottom of the ingredient list, making it easier for people with sensitivities to avoid harmful substances like nuts, dairy, gluten, and soy.

Certifications and Claims

Many food labels also feature various certifications and health claims. These claims may include labels like "organic," "non-GMO," "gluten-free," or "fair trade," and can be useful in making informed choices. However, it's important not to rely solely on these claims as they do not always guarantee a food product is the healthiest option. For example, a product labeled "organic" may still contain high amounts of added sugars, unhealthy fats, or empty calories. Similarly, "gluten-free" products are not automatically healthier, as they may be high in sugar or processed ingredients.

Look for third-party certifications like the USDA Organic seal or the Non-GMO Project Verified label, which ensure that a product meets specific standards for organic farming or non-genetically modified ingredients. These certifications can provide more assurance about the quality of the product but should still be considered alongside the full ingredient list and nutritional facts.

Date Labels

Food labels will often include various date labels, such as "best by," "sell by," or "use by." These dates help indicate when a product is likely to be at its peak quality. However, it's important to know that these dates do not necessarily reflect safety. Many foods are still safe to consume after their "best by" date, though they may have lost some of their flavor or texture. The "sell by" date is used by retailers to know when to remove the product from shelves, but it does not necessarily mean the food is no longer safe. "Use by" dates are typically found on perishable foods and represent the last day a product is guaranteed to be at its best quality.

To minimize food waste, it's important to practice proper storage methods and rely on your senses (sight, smell, and taste) to determine if food is still safe to consume, even after the indicated date.

Understanding Serving Sizes

Serving size is one of the most important aspects of the nutritional label, yet it is often overlooked. Serving sizes are standardized by the FDA, allowing you to compare different products. However, serving sizes do not always reflect how much we actually eat. For example, a bag of chips may list a serving size of 12 chips, but in reality, most people eat far more than that in one sitting. This is why it's crucial to pay attention to the serving size and adjust your calculations based on how much of the product you're consuming. Remember, the nutritional information is based on the serving size provided, so consuming more than one serving means multiplying the nutrients accordingly.

Meal prepping is a powerful strategy to help you stay on track with your health and wellness goals. It allows you to plan and prepare meals in advance, ensuring that you have healthy, nutritious options available throughout the week. By preparing meals ahead of time, you save time, reduce stress, and make healthier decisions that support your lifestyle. This guide will provide you with the essential steps to start meal prepping effectively, so you can enjoy delicious, homemade meals with minimal effort during the week.

1. Plan Your Meals

The first step in meal prepping is planning your meals for the week. Start by deciding which meals you will prepare and how many servings of each you need. Consider breakfast, lunch, dinner, and snacks. It's helpful to have a variety of meals to avoid getting bored, so try to include a mix of proteins, vegetables, grains, and healthy fats. Think about your schedule and determine which days might be busier than others, so you can plan for meals that are quick and easy on those days.

When planning your meals, aim to incorporate a balance of macronutrients: protein, fat, and carbohydrates in each meal. Choose lean proteins such as chicken, turkey, fish, tofu, or legumes, along with whole grains like quinoa, brown rice, or oats. Incorporate healthy fats like avocado, nuts, and olive oil, and be sure to include a variety of colorful vegetables to provide a range of vitamins, minerals, and fiber.

2. Create a Shopping List

Once your meals are planned, it's time to make a shopping list. Go through each recipe and list all the ingredients you will need. Be sure to check your pantry and fridge to see what you already have on hand, so you only purchase what is necessary. Organize your list by categories such as produce, grains, proteins, and dairy (or alternatives), so your shopping trip is more efficient.

When shopping, try to buy in bulk when possible, especially for items like grains, legumes, and frozen vegetables. These ingredients often last longer and can be used in multiple meals throughout the week. Look for fresh, in-season produce to make your meals even more flavorful and nutritious.

3. Prep Your Ingredients

Once you have all your ingredients, it's time to start prepping. Start by washing and chopping your fruits and vegetables. This can be time-consuming but is worth it when it comes to saving time during the week. Chop vegetables like bell peppers, carrots, onions, and zucchini and store them in airtight containers. You can also prepare fruits like berries, grapes, or apples and portion them out for snacks or smoothies.

Next, cook your grains and proteins. If you are making a batch of quinoa, rice, or pasta, cook them in large batches to use throughout the week. For proteins like chicken, turkey, or tofu, season and cook them in large amounts so you can easily incorporate them into different meals. Roasting vegetables is another great way to prepare them in bulk; simply season them with olive oil and your favorite herbs, then roast them in the oven. You can also prepare hard-boiled eggs for a quick and easy snack or to add to salads.

4. Assemble Your Meals

Once all your ingredients are prepped, it's time to assemble your meals. You can either pack individual servings for each day or prepare larger meals to store in the fridge for several days. For example, if you've made a large batch of roasted vegetables, you can combine them with quinoa, grilled chicken, and a healthy dressing for a balanced lunch or dinner. If you prefer to keep meals separate, portion out each ingredient into containers so that you can quickly assemble meals when it's time to eat.

Consider investing in good-quality glass containers that are microwave-safe and have tight-fitting lids. These will keep your meals fresh and make reheating easier. Try to label each container with the meal name and the date it was prepared so you know when to eat it.

5. Store Your Meals Properly

Proper storage is key to keeping your prepped meals fresh throughout the week. Store meals in airtight containers to preserve their flavor and prevent them from spoiling. For meals that you won't eat right away, store them in the fridge for up to 3-4 days. For meals that you want to keep for longer, freeze them in individual portions. Freezing meals can extend their shelf life for weeks, allowing you to enjoy home-cooked meals even when you don't have time to prep.

Make sure to store ingredients separately when possible, especially if you are meal prepping salads or bowls. Keep dressings or sauces in small containers on the side to avoid soggy meals.

6. Reheat and Enjoy

When it's time to eat, simply reheat your prepped meals in the microwave, on the stove, or in the oven. You'll appreciate the time and effort you put into meal prepping when you're able to enjoy a healthy, home-cooked meal without the hassle of cooking from scratch each day. Remember, meal prepping isn't about making every meal perfect, it's about setting yourself up for success and making healthier choices easier.

7. Stay Flexible

While meal prepping is a great way to stay on track, it's important to remain flexible. Life happens, and there may be days when you don't feel like eating what you've prepared, or when something unexpected comes up. If you find that you're craving variety, don't be afraid to switch things up. Keep a few extra ingredients on hand, like frozen vegetables or pre-cooked grains, so you can easily swap out meals if needed.

Meal prepping doesn't have to be rigid or overly complicated. The key is to make it work for you, so it feels like a helpful tool rather than a burden. If you prefer to prep only a few meals for the week instead of everything, that's perfectly fine. The goal is to make healthy eating as convenient as possible, so you're more likely to stick with it long-term.

Made in the USA
Middletown, DE
14 April 2025

73921766R00057